ORCHIDS FOR EVERYONE

ORCHIDS
FOR EVERYONE

BY

O. EIGELDINGER

THE GARDEN BOOK CLUB
121, CHARING CROSS ROAD
LONDON W.C.2

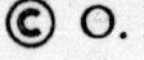

Printed in Great Britain by
BILLING & SONS LTD.
GUILDFORD AND LONDON
H6647

CONTENTS

LIST OF ILLUSTRATIONS

PHOTOGRAPHS

PLATE

LIST OF ILLUSTRATIONS

FOREWORD

The greatly extended, and steadily increasing, interest in the cultivation of orchids is a notable development among modern horticultural activities. There was a time when only wealthy amateurs could afford to get together and maintain a worth-while collection of orchids, but that time has passed and it is now possible for a person of average means to indulge in the most fascinating of floricultural hobbies. This development has led to the publication of many books on the subject, most of them written by commercial and professional growers, whose experience is based on cultural facilities beyond the means of the small grower.

Mr. Eigeldinger has had no professional experience. He is an engineer who, fascinated by the beauty and wide variety of form in orchids, determined to attempt their cultivation. His book is the result of personal experience—trial and error, coupled with keen observation and experiment. What he has accomplished is within the capabilities of any intelligent person who can start with a house 12 ft. by 8 ft. and begin with a few of the most easily managed orchids. Mr. Eigeldinger does all the work himself, but his wife looks after ventilation and shading during his absence from home. He has made many mistakes, overcome them, and now has a collection of plants that not only flourish, but flower freely in their season. He loves his orchids and his intimacy with them is revealed in a book which can be heartily recommended as a friendly and safe guide to potential orchid hobbyists.

July, 1957 CHARLES H. CURTIS, M.B.E., F.L.S., V.M.H.

INTRODUCTION

I HAVE often wondered what would happen if everyone realized that growing orchids for, or even in, their own parlours is within their grasp. Would it cause a buying spree of orchid plants? It may sound fantastic, but it was not so very long ago that the now popular chrysanthemum was considered a novelty and a common or garden tulip bulb sold for £5. True, fantastic prices have been paid for orchid plants in the past which were no better than, nor even as good as, the millions of orchids that have since been raised in our English nurseries. The bulk of these home-raised orchid plants are now marketed at prices within the reach of all but the most unfortunate in our community.

No doubt the high prices paid in the past for "novelties" and plants of outstanding merit, coupled with the erroneous impression that orchids are difficult to grow, have created a very unfavourable atmosphere for the popularization of these beautiful and fascinating flowers. By reporting isolated cases involving the sale of rare "money-spinners," or by giving vent to exaggerated optimism concerning the value of some novelty, the Press quite unwittingly has been feeding this orchids-for-the-rich-only attitude of the public. Meanwhile, discounting this popular fallacy, some of the more enterprising garden hobbyists have been quietly growing orchids in their small conservatories, nine-by-sixes, disused air-raid shelters and living rooms, apparently without the knowledge of the Press.

Judging by the tremendous upsurge the cult of orchid growing has taken during recent years, this most fascinating and gratifying hobby has come to stay, even in the smallest of suburban houses. The evidence of this has been provided by the Amateur Orchid Growers Society, which was started by a dozen enthusiasts some five years ago and now counts over 400 members in all walks of life. Even as I am writing this book, a move is on foot to call into being a national Orchid Society comprising professional growers as well as amateurs.

What, then, is it that makes such enthusiastic devotees of the cult of orchid growing? I will give pride of place to the immense variety of plants the amateur can choose from: he need never have two plants the flowers of which look alike! Secondly, most orchids flower during the winter months! Any gardener who has tried to produce a nice show of home-grown flowers at Christmas, or at any other time during the winter months, will readily appreciate this welcome turn of Mother Nature. Thirdly, the plants, given suitable conditions, last and multiply indefinitely and thus become individuals whose likes and dislikes it is a pleasure to study. I have in my collection plants that were raised fifty years ago. Ease of culture and extreme adaptability of orchid plants seldom fail to spur the amateur on to increase and improve his collection. Add to that the conviction that he is growing something worth while, which can be shared and enjoyed by all the family, and you have the picture of a typical amateur orchid grower!

Now I want to make it clear that I am an *amateur* orchid grower, writing in the light of my own experiences in pursuing this fascinating hobby. My recommendations do not always coincide with the professional or the orthodox method of orchid culture, and the reasons for any deviation from accepted standards will be given as occasion arises. Orchids are very accommodating creatures and totally opposed methods of culture can ultimately lead to the same results. That is all in favour of the amateur and particularly of the novice. Due allowance also is made for the likelihood of the owner of the collection being away from home all day, and often for longer periods, with nobody in attendance.

The conditions under which orchids are grown vary so considerably according to the type of house or structure, locality, type of soil on which the house is built, etc., that no hard-and-fast rules can be laid down and much must be left to the observation of the amateur. This is particularly the case where orchids are grown in glass frames in the living room. Whilst the novice may at first prefer to have cut-and-dried information on the various aspects of culture, he will in time find his new hobby all the more interesting by bringing into play the results of his own observations.

It is not the purpose of this book to catalogue a large number of subjects to be gathered into a comprehensive collection, but rather to help the novice to avoid the pitfalls and to make a success of a limited number of genera known to be amenable to easy culture. An enthusiastic amateur is apt to acquire as many genera as he can, irrespective of their cultural requirements, only to find that he cannot flower more than half his plants. By limiting his choice to one or two genera, for which he can provide suitable conditions, he soon learns to familiarize himself with them and can rely on a fine floral display instead. I will therefore confine my recommendations to genera which I myself have grown successfully for many years.

The photographs of plants and flowers in this book have all been taken from my own collection, except in the case of cymbidium flowers and one or two others flowering too late for publication in this book. The source of borrowed photographs is gratefully acknowledged in each case.

September, 1956

O. EIGELDINGER
Twickenham

1

HOUSING

GENERAL REMARKS

THIS is by far the most important chapter, for on the type and aspect of the house available or to be built, will depend the choice of plants, amount of attention required, running costs, etc. Whilst existing greenhouses can usually be modified to ensure success with orchids, the budding orchidist will be better off by replacing dilapidated structures or houses with glass down to the ground, and thus give his new hobby a better chance. A disused garage, or air-raid shelter, with a glass roof has been known to give better results and far less trouble than many a glasshouse marketed today. Although most orchids have originated from countries with tropical climates, it must not be assumed that they thrive in the full glare of the sun; on the contrary, few orchids grow under such conditions. The natural abode of epiphytic orchids is on the lower branches of trees, shielded from the sun by the overhanging branches, whilst the terrestrial orchids are usually found growing in wooded undergrowths and crevices. It follows therefore that orchids grown in cultivation under glass must be provided with adequate shading from direct sunlight. The need for shading during bright weather, coupled with the high temperature conductivity of glass, with resultant loss of heat in cold weather, makes glass appear an expensive luxury.

The type of houses or structures suitable for orchid growing may vary considerably. Let no one assume that special structures are needed in which to grow orchids. I myself started growing orchids in a mass-produced span-roof type greenhouse, built of wood with side lights, measuring 9 feet by 6 feet, and the results obtained from it were sufficiently encouraging for me to embark on the building of a larger house, although of a different type. The trouble with these mass-produced glasshouses with wood bases, side lights and ventilators is that neither heat nor atmospheric moisture can be retained for any length of time, unless it be in the summer when it often becomes impossible to keep the thermometer reading down to a reasonable level. As many amateurs have to depend on this or a similar type of house, I will list a few modifications that can be easily carried out by the owner to counteract its drawbacks.

LINING OLD HOUSES

Line all the four sides, including side ventilators, which are superfluous, with asbestos sheeting screwed to the glazing bars, from the eaves down to the floor, not forgetting the door, which of course has to be done separately. If the cavities between the boards and glass and the asbestos are filled in with glass wool, so much the better. That will still give your plants more light through the glass roof than they require. Then line the glass roof with a web of Windolite or Polythene sheeting (preferably 0·005 in. thick), tacked on the glazing bars with brass drawing-pins or narrow strips of wood. Leave a gap near the lower edge of the roof ventilator (which, in any case, is usually too large for our purpose). Make sure there are no "bags" or wrinkles in the lining material before pinning, otherwise the condensation will collect there and drop in the wrong places. Needless to say, all the woodwork should be repainted before carrying out the covering-up operations. You will be surprised what difference this simple and inexpensive modification makes in the atmospheric condition in the house, and to find that your minimum temperature reading has gone up by some 10°F. with the same expenditure of fuel. Your "coolhouse" may thus become an intermediate house, giving you a wider scope in your choice of plants. Similarly, it will help you to keep the temperature within bounds in hot summer weather, provided, of course, the usual shading has been applied outside—*i.e.*, above the roof. This latter problem will be dealt with under the heading "Shading."

2

BUILDING YOUR OWN ORCHID HOUSE

TYPE AND ASPECT OF HOUSE

THIS chapter is for those lucky enough to build their own orchid house. I use the word "lucky," because it gives the owner a chance to build a house that will save him a lot of work and attention, which is appreciated most by those whose work takes them away from home. The ideal orchid house is the one that carries with it the best insulation against outside weather conditions, cuts down attention to a minimum and is economical to run on the score of fuel consumption.

I prefer the lean-to type of house to the span-roof type for two reasons: (*a*) there is only one set of blinds to be operated instead of two; and (*b*) the high wall of the lean-to allows for a tiered staging to accommodate many more plants than would be possible under the eaves of the span-roof type, unless this is wide enough to allow for a central stage.

The aspect of the house often has to conform to the available space and layout of the garden and other outbuildings, but an east to west run has decided advantages. The north (high) side of the lean-to needs no shading at all and only from June to September in the case of a span-roof house. During the winter months, when the sun is most precious for the welfare of our charges, the whole of the house gets the benefit from its scanty rays and there are no "dark ends."

MATERIAL

The walls should be built of bricks or breeze blocks, the latter rendered with cement up to the eaves, topped by a wall plate firmly bolted into the wall. The most suitable wood is Canadian Red Cedar, often referred to as Western Red Cedar. It should be first quality—*i.e.*, notchless material. This hardwood does not need painting, although a good soaking with linseed oil before assembly and a coating with varnish after erection is recommended. The job of periodic painting inside and outside is not one to be looked forward to, even if one knew where to house the plants in the meantime. Furthermore, unlike other hardwoods, red cedar is known to be immune from woodworm and very easy to work on. Use 24-oz. horticultural glass, which is readily obtainable. Lighter than 24-oz. glass is given to sag and therefore not recommended.

DOUBLE GLAZING

This subject of double glazing has come very much to the fore in recent times, at least in this country, where the fuel costs have risen enormously since the war. On the Continent double glazing has been practised in living houses from time immemorial, and many double-glazed greenhouses are in evidence, so it is by no means a new fad or invention. Whilst the saving in fuel effected by double glazing is considerable in an orchid house, it brings in its wake many more equally important advantages which are not so obvious, except to the grower who has had experience with both single- and double-glazed houses. Perhaps my own experience will serve as a guidance to those who are wavering on the brink of double glazing and who are possibly concerned about the extra cost involved.

By replacing my single-glazed metal structure with a double-glazed Western Red Cedar frame I have cut the cost of heating by half! This means that my new structure will be paid for in three to four years by the saving effected in fuel. On this score alone the change-over from single to double glazing has been worth while. What I consider of even greater consequence is the marked improvement in the atmospheric conditions. Gone is the sudden drop in temperature on a sunny day followed by a chilly evening. Gone also are the hot pipes with their drying effect upon plants and surroundings. Even on a frosty night I can still bear my hands on the pipes for as long as I wish to. The result is a pleasantly humid atmosphere, day and night, whatever the weather conditions outside.

The only arguments against double glazing I have had to counter so far came from people with no experience with double glazing. Objections were raised by glasshouse manufacturers in an attempt to justify their apparent unwillingness to tackle the problems connected with manufacture. The main objection is that of increased condensation. Obviously if the moisture cannot escape, as it only too easily does through a single-glazed structure, it must remain in the house and eventually settle on the roof glass. This is not a drawback, as commonly assumed, but a blessing in disguise. If the moisture can escape through the roof, so can the warmth, necessitating frequent damping down and stoking of the fire, unless thermostatically controlled electricity or gas does the job for you, but whatever it is, it will still cost you money to replace lost heat. Another argument frequently met with, is increased heat in the summer. In actual fact, the opposite is the case, since the air cushion between the two panes of glass acts as insulator. The problem of condensation will be dealt with under its appropriate heading.

Whilst the claims I have made in favour of double glazing may sound fantastic or overrated, they are based on my own observations arising from facts and figures, and my only regret is that it has taken me eighteen years of single-glazed house management before I ventured into the field of double glazing. I am so sure of my facts that I venture to prophesy that in a few years' time single-glazed structures will be as rare as double-glazed ones are today, at least where orchids are concerned.

SHAPE AND SIZE OF THE HOUSE

When considering the size of the house to be built, bear in mind that orchid houses have a habit of becoming too small in a few years' time. That is the experience of most of us who have added extensions to the existing houses. You cannot be too ambitious when considering the size of the structure—and it invariably pays in the long run. The same applies to the height of the house, for the greater the air space the easier it is to control the atmosphere. Any owner of a small prefabricated greenhouse, with eaves only about 18 inches above the stage, must be aware of the difficulty of keeping the inside temperature down to a reasonable limit on a hot summer's day. Furthermore, he could stage twice the number of plants within the same width and breadth if only he had higher walls! The lessons to be drawn from these circumstances obviously indicate the desirability for higher walls, even at the expense of roof slope or angle. The only reason I can see for the steep roofs on the standard type greenhouse, is the disposal of condensation at the eaves. That surely is too high a price to pay for the object in view, which can be achieved by a simple and inexpensive dodge, as suggested under the heading "Condensation."

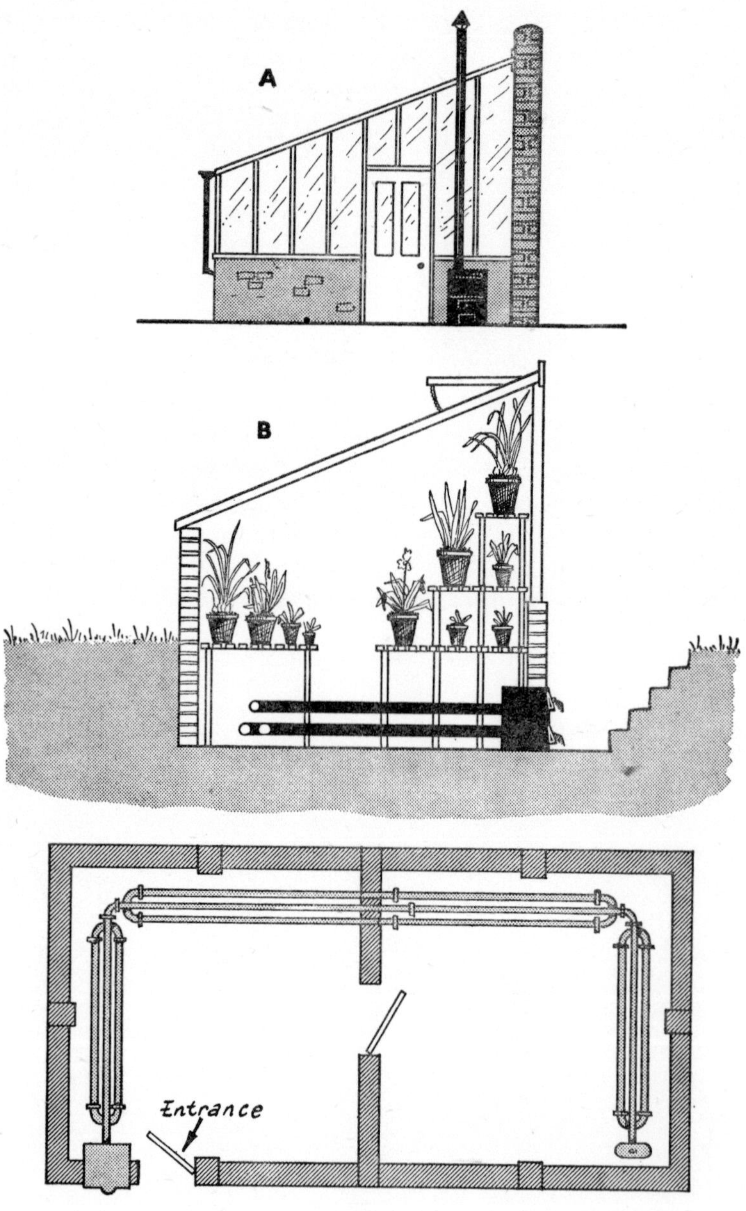

FIG. 1 A. LEAN-TO "POPULAR" TYPE BUILT AGAINST EXISTING WALL. B. LEAN-TO BUILT FOR ORCHID CULTURE STANDING ON ITS OWN. C. PLAN OF ONE OF THE AUTHOR'S LEAN-TO TYPE HOUSES.

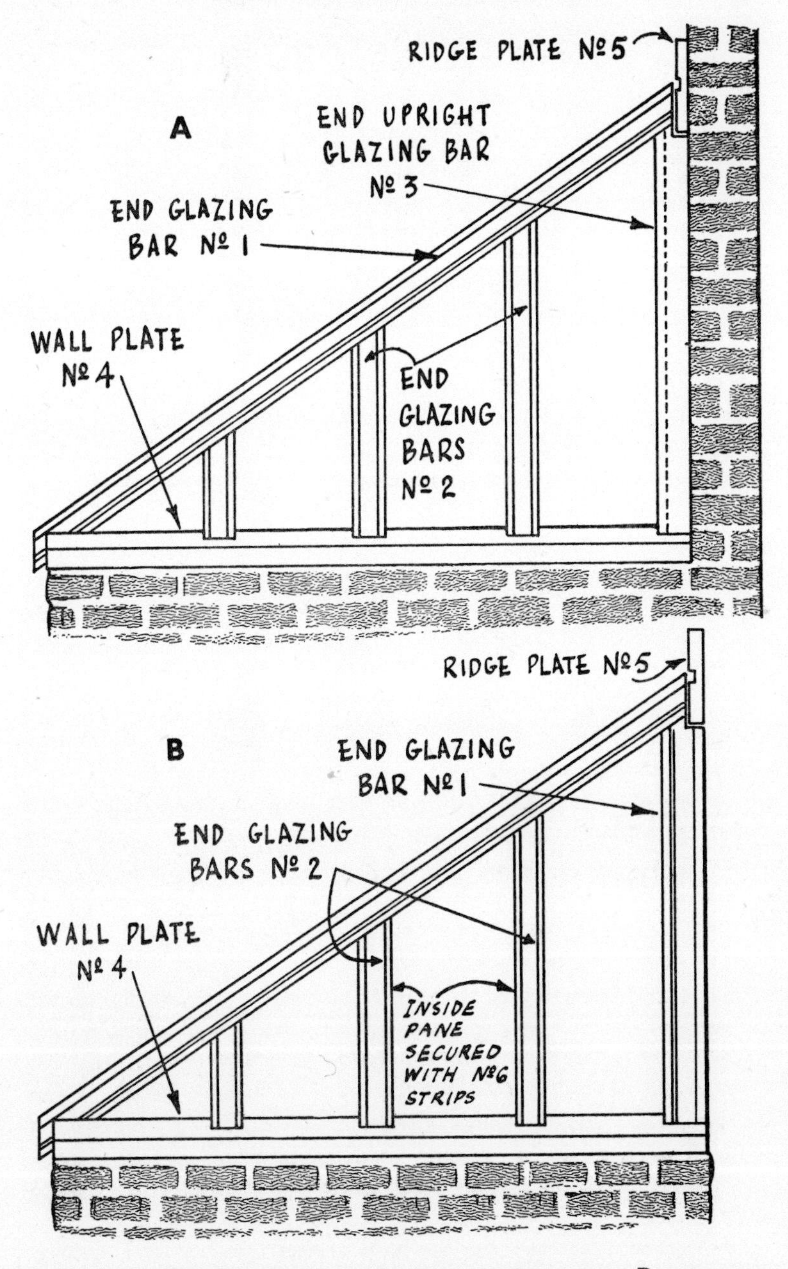

FIG. 2 A. SIDE LIGHT OF LEAN-TO BUILT AGAINST EXISTING WALL. B. SIDE LIGHT OF LEAN-TO STANDING ON ITS OWN.

LEAN-TO TYPE

As already stated, I favour the lean-to type house, but the method of construction and machining of the wood are essentially the same for a span-roof house, and in either case can easily be carried out by anyone handy with protractor and saw. If the outside appearance of the house is of any consequence, I suggest a roof gable with double-glazed back and triangular sides, the roof resting directly on the brick wall in the front (assuming that the lowest part of the roof represents the front of the house). The wall should be not less than 5 feet high, with another 3 or 4 feet high double-glazed wood frame at the back or higher end. That brings the house to a height of 8 ft. 6 in. or 9 ft. 6 in. outside measurement, and if that is too high from an æsthetic point of view, or infringing the local by-laws, the floor of the house can always be dropped a couple of feet by excavation. In point of fact I have done so in my own case, not for either of the cited reasons, but, being situated on gravel soil, it helps to retain a moist floor as well as warmth. A raised cement path runs between the stages on either side and discarded potting compost under the stage prevents the water draining away too quickly. The odontoglossum house, however, is cemented all over, and, against copious advice to the contrary, I have found the cement floor a more efficient help for controlling the moisture content in the atmosphere than an earth floor.

As will be seen from the illustrations, a 2-inch gap is maintained throughout between the two panes of glass. The sockets or rebates in the wallplate along the front or low end of the house need only be ¼ inch deep, as the ends of the glazing bars are cut to fit the slope of the wallplate according to the angle of the roof. Three-inch brass screws should be used and the holes for it bored with a drill gun, as well as the countersink holes to bring the screwheads below the surface level of the wood. The moulded supports (No. 6) for the lower pane are most conveniently cut to 28-inch length, butted together and secured with two brass screws to the glazing bar. The outer panes of glass are embedded in putty and secured with brads and should overlap about ¾ inch. The inner panes do not overlap and are butted together. Make sure, therefore, that the glass is cut square.

A purlin, supported in the middle by a galvanized 1½-inch diameter scaffolding tube, will prevent any sagging of the roof even if plants are hung up on the glazing bars. This purlin should

PLATE I

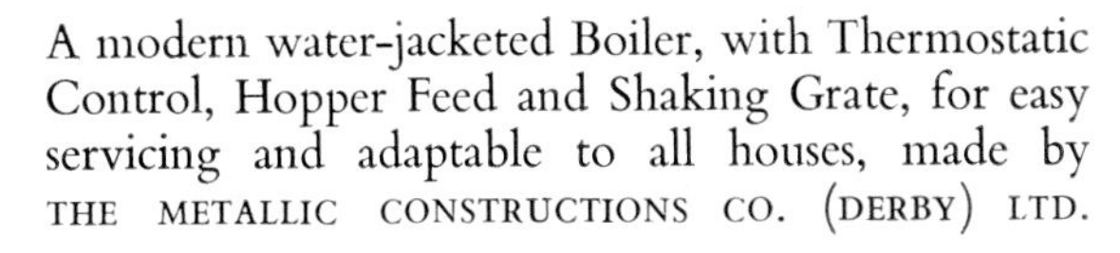

A modern water-jacketed Boiler, with Thermostatic Control, Hopper Feed and Shaking Grate, for easy servicing and adaptable to all houses, made by THE METALLIC CONSTRUCTIONS CO. (DERBY) LTD.

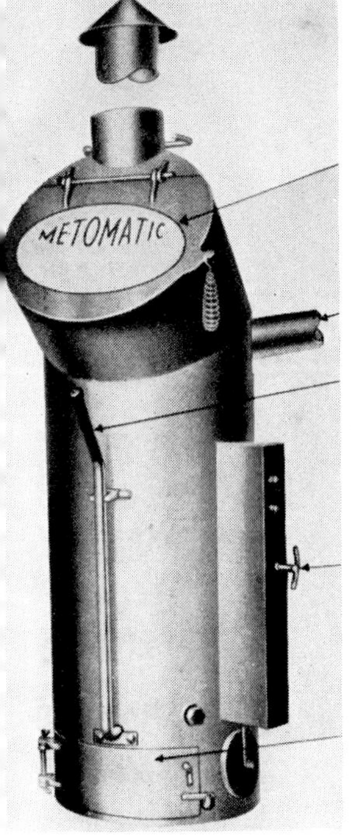

PLATE II (*right*)
CTC Oil Burner "Junior"

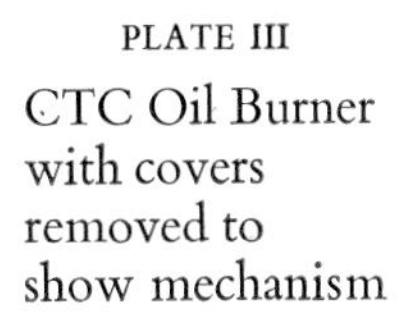

PLATE III
CTC Oil Burner with covers removed to show mechanism

PLATE IV. Conversion Unit for gas with Burner outside

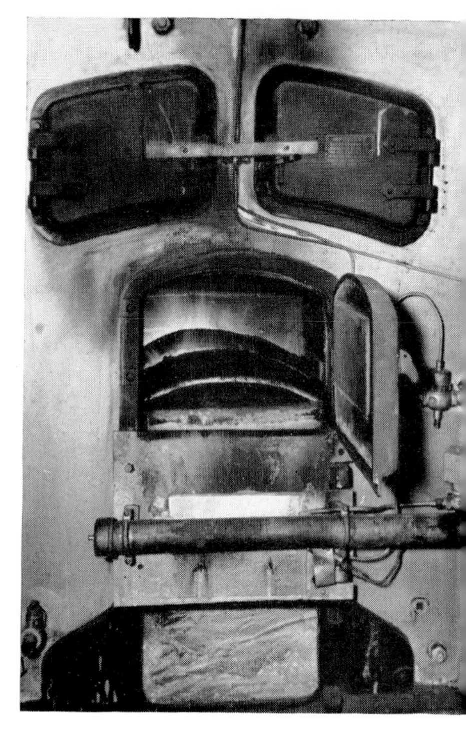

PLATE V. Conversion Unit for gas showing Combustion Chamber with Domed Fire-brick Top

PLATE VI. Extension Pipe with Heating Element thermostatically controlled and additional to Boiler

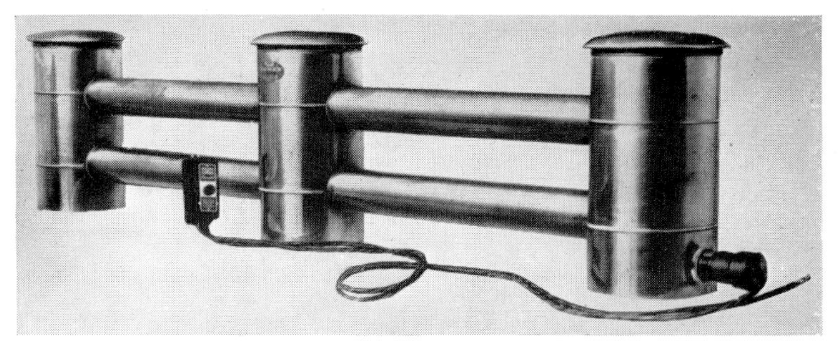

PLATE VII. "Humex" Portable Electric Heater

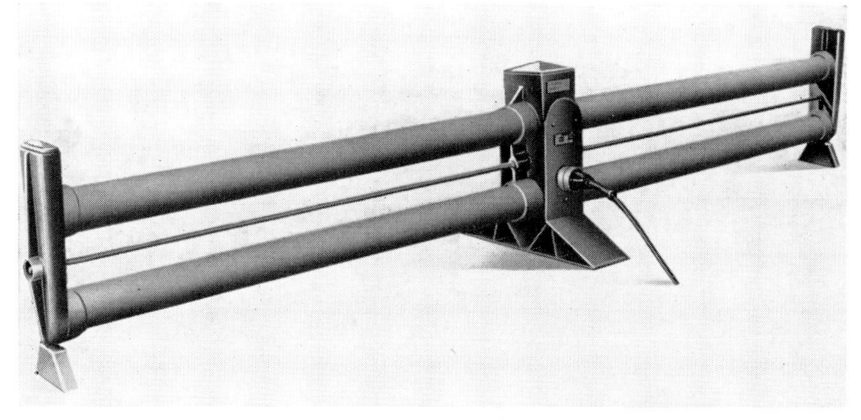

PLATE VIII. "Remploy" Portable Electric Heater

PLATE IX. Underside of Double Glazed Roof showing Windolite Anti-Drip Webbing

PLATE X. Simple Ventilator Raising Gear allowing for fine adjustment

PLATE XI. Lath Blinds on the Cattleya House

PLATE XII. Pinolium Split Pine Blinds on Odontoglossum House

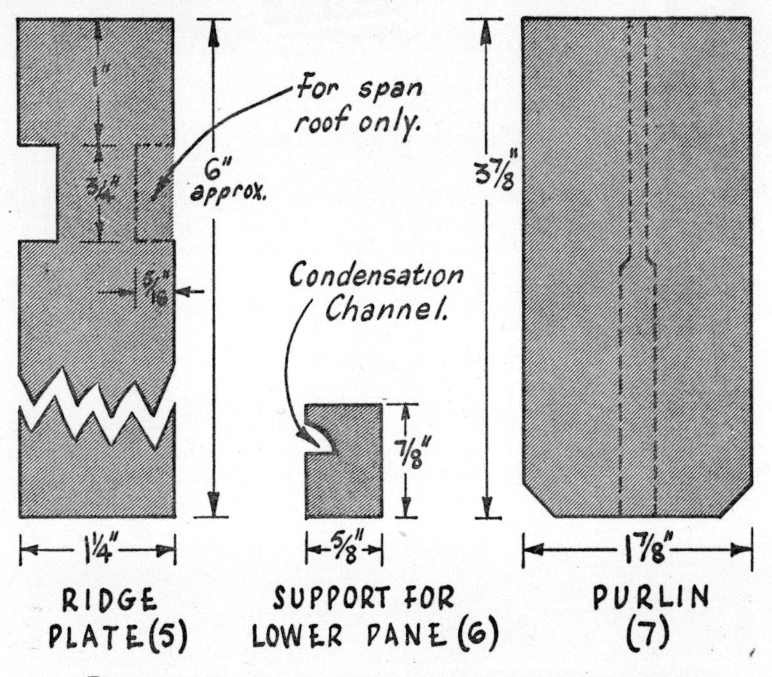

FIG. 3 SECTION OF RIDGE PLATE, PURLIN AND SUPPORTING STRIPS.

be rested on the two end walls and screwed to each glazing bar in between with 3-inch brass screws, for which bores and counter-bores are drilled through the purlin, as indicated by the dotted lines on sketch 7. The scaffolding tube supporting the purlin in the middle is threaded at one end with a 3-inch round nut, with which subsequent adjustments in height can be conveniently made.

WATER STORAGE

Rainwater being essential for the well-being of the plants, adequate provision must be made for the storage of rainwater. The general practice is to run guttering along the eaves, with a conduit through the brick wall which carries the water from the roof into a cement-lined concrete tank sunk into the ground. This has much to commend itself, but has its drawbacks. In time the water in the tank gets polluted and the latter needs emptying and cleaning out. Again, the melting snow will feed this tank and chill the water, unless the tank can be accommodated

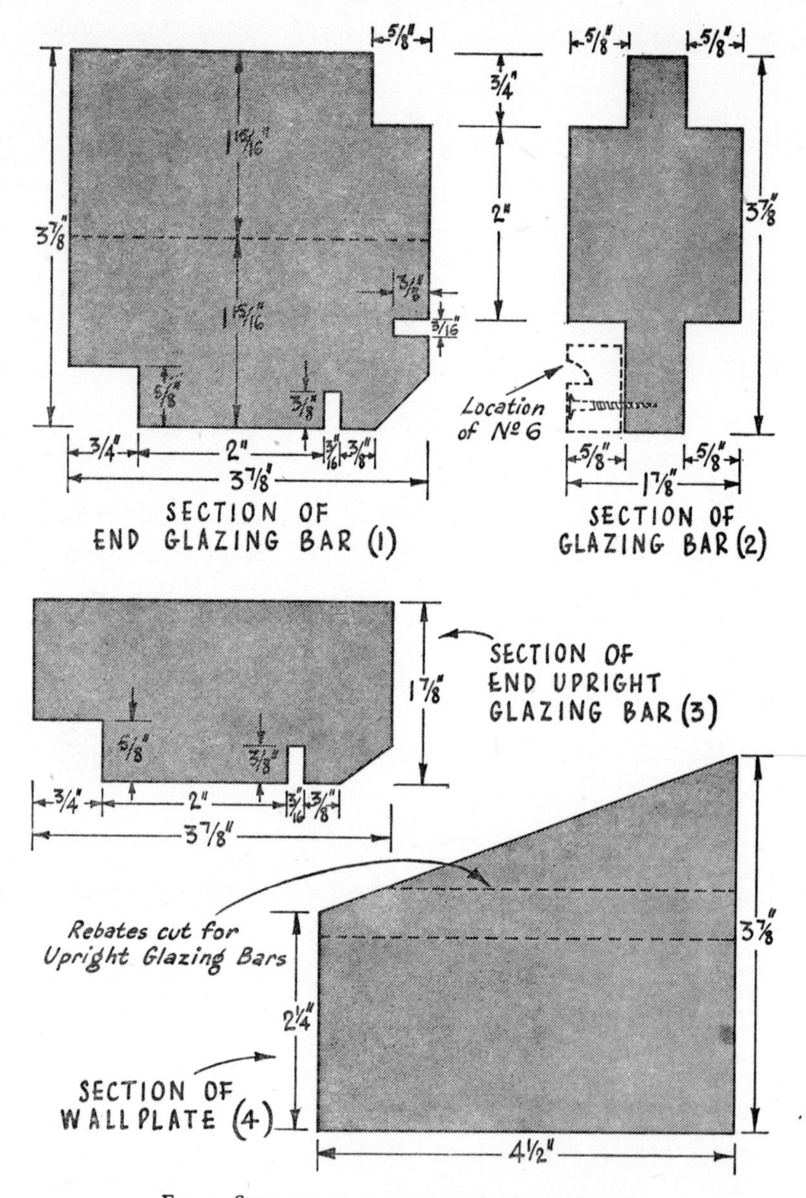

FIG. 4 SECTIONS OF GLAZING BARS AND WALLPLATE.

near the boiler. It just would not do to chill the roots every time water is administered to the plants.

To overcome these drawbacks, I had a movable galvanized iron tank made, with a draw-off tap near the bottom, as well as three smaller vitreous enamel tanks, one for each section. The latter are stationed near the heating pipes and fed from the former, either via a rubber hose connected to the tap or by carrying the water in a bucket. The smaller tanks are used for watering the plants and can easily be cleaned out and, of course, are always refilled *after* watering, to ensure the water being tepid at the time of use.

SHADING MATERIAL

The most popular and cheapest form of shading is the application, either by brush or spray gun, of lime and starch or other mixtures, which is commonly referred to as "permanent shading." There are a number of branded mixtures on the market which are preferable to the home-made concoctions, more convenient to use and not so likely to wash into the water tank. I have tried most of these branded distempers as well as some of my own, but none has proved, in my opinion, so satisfactory as a quite recent introduction—viz., "Videnor" orchid shading, in green and white, obtainable from W. S. Birch and Co. Ltd., Aldbro' Works, Scott Street, Hull.

"Permanent shading," which is, of course, all but permanent, has its advantages as well as its drawbacks. It is cheaper than any other form of shading and there is no damage through forgetfulness or wrong weather prognostication. If the owner, or an understudy, is in constant attendance, he is not likely to err on that score, but what of the owner who is away from his orchids all day (poor chap)? Is he to pull the blinds over before leaving on a dull or rainy morning or take a chance and leave them off? I have done both and lived through some anxious moments in consequence.

Despite these considerations I plump for the pull-over blinds, whether operated by cords, or rolled sideways, as these enable the owner to take prevailing weather conditions into account—at least while somebody is in attendance. For the cattleya and cymbidium houses I prefer lath blinds of Western Red Cedar, and for the odontoglossum and cypripedium houses I recommend Pinolium blinds (painted split pine). The latter give a better light diffusion and heat dispersal than the lath blinds, which would require additional shading for the last two sections. Canvas blinds are a poor substitute and soon wear out.

STAGING

In the case of the conventional span-roof house the possibilities of staging are reduced to a horizontal stage along the three sides, unless the house is 14 feet or more in width, in which case a tiered centre stage can be added to the side stages, with a path running in between. The lean-to type of house however has, by its very nature, a high wall, against which stages can be erected in tiers from 12 inches from the floor to within 18 inches of the roof. The individual steps or tiers need only be about 10 inches wide and the same distance apart, with a couple of inches either way added where cymbidiums are grown. This arrangement can easily provide double the amount of space of a horizontal stage.

Some growers consider a covered stage, or additional moisture-retaining stage, imperative for growing orchids. This was particularly so in the old days, when patterns were more rigidly adhered to than they are today, and when the cost of fuel was low enough to ignore wastage. The idea of a covered or moisture stage, as opposed to the slatted or open stage, is to help in the creation of a moist atmosphere. Unfortunately, as I have found out to my cost, it does not end there. Much heat is trapped below the stage, as evidenced by the flourishing state of my tradescantias, begonia rex and other foliage plants growing under the moisture staging. It was by sheer accident that I found out this discrepancy, dropping the thermometer accidentally (fortunately on soft ground) after reading the temperature among the cattleyas, which then stood at a very unsatisfactory 56° F. Thinking that the thermometer was not worth picking up any more, I left it on the floor for a few minutes, to be swept up later. Imagine my surprise when I found it intact, with a temperature reading of 68° F.

This is the sort of temperature I would like my orchids to grow in, so off came the moisture stage! The cattleyas responded magnificently and started to grow at a much faster pace. I repeated the process in the cypripedium house, with similar results, and when I subsequently built the odontoglossum house I provided only an open slatted stage. The thermostats for the first two sections were then reset at several degrees lower for the sake of economy and the plants above the stage still revelled in a minimum of 60° F.

What of the moisture in the atmosphere? I have more than a suspicion that too much is made of atmospheric moisture for orchids, but this will be dealt with in a later chapter. In my opinion enough moisture can be created by damping down the floor, and easily too much where double glazing exists. The warmth of the pipes freely circulating among the plants tends to dry the latter out quicker, with beneficial effect, and in any case the pipes will not have to be so hot to warm the air above the staging.

VENTILATION

Like all living things, orchids must have an adequate supply of fresh air to help in their assimilation process. It is a safe guess, however, that the owner, or attendant, uses up more of this commodity in a small house than his plants do, especially if he is, like myself, an inveterate pipe smoker! The chances are that a single-glazed structure admits as much fresh air as his plants actually require, even when the ventilators are closed. You have only to stand below a closed ventilator on a cold day to appreciate what I mean. Every ventilator in the house can be looked upon as a potential trap-door, through which heat is either lost or gained, according to the outside weather conditions. The orchid grower's aim is to retain as much artificial heat when the outside temperature is below the requirements of his plants and to exclude as much of the natural heat as possible when the position is reversed—*i.e.*, in hot weather.

It follows, therefore, that the fewer and smaller the ventilators, the better the control that can be exercised on the inside atmospheric conditions. For obvious reasons, the ventilators are kept closed during cold weather, whilst in hot summer weather you cannot reduce the inside temperature by opening the vents. The only means of reducing the inside temperature I know of is through shading, apart from creating artificial draughts, which is inimical to the well-being of your plants.

When I designed my new double-glazed structure, I reduced the size of the ventilators to 18 inches square, one in each section, and discovered since then that half their size would have been sufficient for the needs of the plants. As it is, my ventilators are never open more than 3 to 4 inches. Mechanically operated ventilator control gear is an advantage, inasmuch as fine adjustments can be made by the turn of a handle. Automatic control gear operated by thermostats has an appeal to the owner who is away from home a great deal, but it defeats its own object in hot weather. With this type, the ventilators open automatically with the rise of the inside temperature, which would be quite in order for the greater part of the year, but not in hot summer weather. Automation, therefore, seems to have its limits where orchids are concerned, which is just as well, as the enthusiastic orchidist likes to fuss around a bit!

CONDENSATION

The bugbear of condensation has influenced greenhouse design more than any other single factor. It has given us the traditional span-roof house with high ridge and low eaves, the roof thus almost falling down to stage level. With anything less than a 45° roof slope, the atmospheric moisture, which is bound to condense on the roof glass while the ventilators are closed, would fall in drips of condensation on the plants below, particularly below the overlaps of the roof panes. This is particularly the case in an orchid house, where the ventilators remain closed for longer periods than they can be left open sufficiently to dry up the condensation on the glass.

With double glazing this problem is even more accentuated, since the atmospheric moisture cannot escape as freely as it can through the overlaps of a single-glazed roof. This to me appears the most likely explanation for the reluctance of the glasshouse manufacturers to supply double-glazed houses. Valuable inside space is thus sacrificed to escape the evils of drips from condensation, yet a simple dodge can neutralise the whole problem of condensation!

In orchid houses we have to accept condensation not as an evil apparition but as a blessing in disguise, since atmospheric moisture plays a great part in the growth and natural development of the plants. Our problem is therefore reduced to providing a channel for the droplets of condensation falling from the roof. The photograph Plate IX shows sections of the roof lined with a web of Windolite, one above and one below the purlin. Instead of Windolite it could be Polythene or other transparent material which does not obstruct the ingress of ultra-violet rays. The webs are stretched from side to side and pinned on the glazing bars with brass drawing-pins. A gap is left above each web to allow the moisture in the atmosphere to rise above the web and to settle on the glass, whence it will fall in drips on to the web. A light aluminium channel will take away the water from condensation from the web above the purlin to the side walls, whilst the web below the purlin will take the water to the eaves.

As the reader will gather from the photographs, my lean-to house has very little roof fall, and condensation would have been a very real problem in this double-glazed structure had it not been for the simple dodge described above. This has given me a chance to make optimum use of the "low" wall at the eave, as well as of the side walls.

3

HEATING

WHATEVER the size of the orchid house, the aim should be to spread the heat over as wide an area as possible, rather than concentrate its source in any one convenient place. The most effective answer to this problem is water or steam pipes running along three of the four sides of the house, fed by a stove located outside the plant house, preferably in a covered boiler house built for the purpose, which can most conveniently be used as a potting shed. Such an installation may, however, prove too costly for a small house and other means have to be resorted to. In such a case electricity will provide the easiest and most convenient solution, as there are no fumes to contend with and practically no attention is required.

PORTABLE UNITS

Dealing with portable units first, an excellent stove, marketed under the name of "Humex," of the immersion heater type, can quite effectively take the place of an outside stove with heating pipes—at least in a small house. If two of these portable "Humex" stoves can be installed, one on either side, the whole area of a small house is covered by the heat radiation of the 7-feet long water pipes. Alternatively, additional tubular dry heaters can be fitted to the walls farthest from the "Humex" heater, with good effect. My only objection to tubular dry heaters is the fierce heat they give off and their comparatively high running cost. With the immersion heater, the water remains hot for a long time, thus conserving the heat produced by the element, whereas the tubular dry heater turns cold in a matter of minutes after switching off or cutting out of the current by the thermostat.

OIL

Blue flame and other paraffin oil heaters are on the market in variety, but unless they have an outlet for the fumes through the roof, I would only entertain their use in orchid houses as an emergency measure. As such, I have used paraffin stoves myself during and after the war, when power cuts were the order of the day (and sometimes of the night too), but was glad enough to dispense with these when alternative means of heating became available. Oil burners are bound to burn up the oxygen in a confined space, for which reason some ventilation must be left on all the time, and one mistake or neglect may cost you a week's holiday cleaning the place out and sponging the soot off every leaf of the plants! Furthermore, if you cultivate and appreciate scented orchids (and who doesn't), you are more likely to get the smell of paraffin up your nostrils than the exquisite perfume of scented orchids!

PERMANENT UNITS

For the permanent heating installation there are four possibles:

(1) Solid fuel combustion.
(2) Fuel oil.
(3) Gas heating.
(4) Electricity.

Whichever method or means one may prefer, thermostatic control, by means of a room thermostat in the plant house itself, should be provided as a matter of course. Be as generous as you can when deciding on the number of heating pipes, as this will affect your management of the house more than anything else. The choice of the type of heating must depend on many factors, such as:

(*a*) Initial cost of the installation.
(*b*) Subsequent running costs.
(*c*) Attention required.
(*d*) Storage facilities for fuel.
(*e*) Accessibility for supplies.
(*f*) Provision for possible extensions.
(*g*) Provision for breakdowns.
(*h*) Dependability of supplies.

No doubt you can think of other circumstances that might influence the choice, but it would be unwise to ignore any one of the points enumerated above. I nearly slipped up myself on deciding on the type of heating by leaving out of consideration (*e*), the accessibility for supplies. Plans were available for the installation of a crude oil combustion unit, when I discovered at the last moment that the path between house and outbuildings was not wide enough for rolling in the oil drums, without first carrying out extensive demolition and reconstruction work!

(1) *Solid Fuel Combustion*

The coke and anthracite boiler has held its ground for a very long time, but in recent years other forms of heating have encroached on its popularity. One reason for the decline in popularity is the uncertainty of fuel supplies and another reason the disproportionate rise in the cost of solid fuels. The heat output cannot be controlled in the same way or anywhere near as accurately as with oil, gas or electricity. As a result, orchid houses heated by solid fuels nearly always register a higher temperature during mild or sunny spells than those heated by one of the three alternatives. For considerations of safety it is necessary to keep the boiler going at times when no heating is required or desirable. The margin of economy is thereby whittled down to a negligible quantity and insufficient to compensate for handling, stoking and disposal of clinkers and ashes. The layout and arrangement of pipes are similar in all forms of heating and the following sketch can serve as a basis.

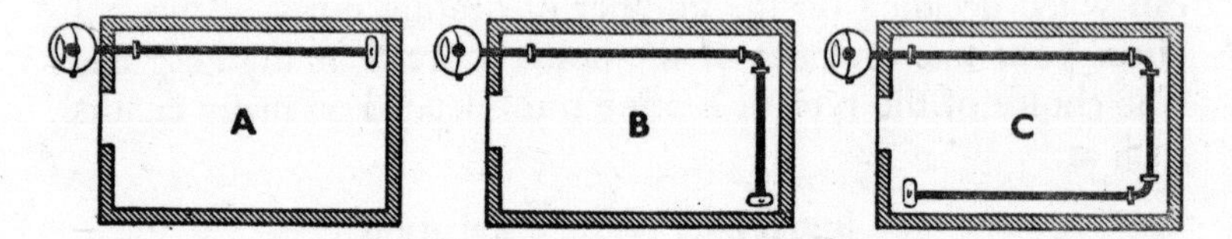

FIG. 5 LAY-OUT PLAN FOR THREE ALTERNATIVE HEATING ARRANGEMENTS.

(2) *Oil Combustion Units*

Of the various types of heating, this is the only one I have had no personal experience with. The information I have gathered on this subject and observation of such heating units in operation are, however, sufficiently encouraging to envisage this form of heating. The most relevant claim made for oil combustion is its economical use, no doubt the cheapest form of greenhouse heating. The thermostatic control, so essential to the well-being of orchids during the owner's absence, responds in the same way as electricity and gas. Like the latter, it eliminates the tedium of stoking and handling, with the additional advantage of quick reaction with fluctuating temperatures.

Existing solid fuel boilers can easily be converted to oil combustion, special conversion units being manufactured to operate in conjunction with existing installations. Such a conversion unit is offered by the C.T.C. Heat (London) Ltd. of 17, Sloane Street, London, S.W.1, in various capacities at a reasonable cost.

Plate II shows the complete apparatus, except the supply tank and thermostat, which are installed inside the greenhouse, comprising:

(*a*) C.T.C. oil burner.
(*b*) Face plate to replace the doors of the boiler to take the burner.
(*c*) Oil tank with oil level gauge, sludge cock, filler pipe, vent pipe and take-off tapping.
(*d*) ½-inch black iron pipe line connecting oil tank to burner, with two stop cocks.
(*e*) Electric wiring to wire up controls and thermostat.
(*f*) Automatic fire valve operated by a fusible link, with a melting-point of 150° F.

For maximum conductivity and radiation of heat, a refractory brick lining has to be fitted inside existing boilers, which the makers undertake as part of their installation job.

The oil burner is controlled by thermostats and electronic panel, so that its function is completely automatic. It atomizes the oil, mixing it with air in the right proportion to create soot-free, smokeless combustion.

(3) *Gas Heating*

Heating of greenhouses by gas is not something that has achieved the popularity it deserves, but it has been successfully tried out. Provided the gas mains are within a short distance from the greenhouse, the cost of the installation lies within reasonable limits even for the small house. The efficiency of the modern gas boiler is unexcelled by any other form of heating, and maintenance is restricted to once-yearly cleaning. The running-cost is on a par with that of electricity, with the added advantage of a quicker "up-take" and the practical elimination of failures.

Anyone with a solid fuel boiler can have it converted to gas heating—as I have done—with a few modifications and, of course, the installation of burners and safety devices. Plate IV shows some of the apparatus which forms part of the conversion unit in my boiler house, but it cannot be said that it can be run as economically as a properly constructed gas boiler.

In the specially constructed gas boiler, the baffling arrangement for trapping the heat output is so designed that loss of heat is almost completely eliminated. If desired, an electrically operated room thermostat can take the place of the gas operated thermostat, in which case no gas leads are needed inside the house. Plate V and Fig. 6 show a typical gas boiler, working in conjunction with hot-water pipes.

Special two-part tariff rates are available and anyone interested should contact their nearest branch of the Gas Board, who will co-operate with the enquirer to the fullest extent possible.

(4) *Electricity*

Electricity offers the choice of two types of heat generation—viz., by dry heating element and by the immersion type of element. The former can be very useful as a stand-by for supplementing other forms of heating in very cold weather, and for taking over in conjunction with thermostatic control after the boiler or other apparatus has been stopped, especially during the spring and autumn months. For the permanent type of heater I prefer the immersion element in conjunction with hot-water pipes, for the reasons already stated.

Although representing a most convenient heating method, electricity alone, without any alternative method of heating, is somewhat risky. There are several possibilities that can cause your electricity to fail, and when it does so it is not likely to be at a time when you can conveniently deal with it! More likely than not you will have to wait for a qualified electrician to turn up and to locate the cause of the trouble for you, before anything can be done. It might be a burnt-out element, or a short in the circuit, or a defect in the relay box or in the thermostat, or just a "tired" fuse. Whatever it is can take too long to put right, even if you have taken the precaution of keeping spares of all the components. On such occasions it will save you a lot of worries and possible losses if you have an alternative to fall back on. In my case, electricity was the alternative to solid fuel combustion first and then to gas, which took over from the former. Having

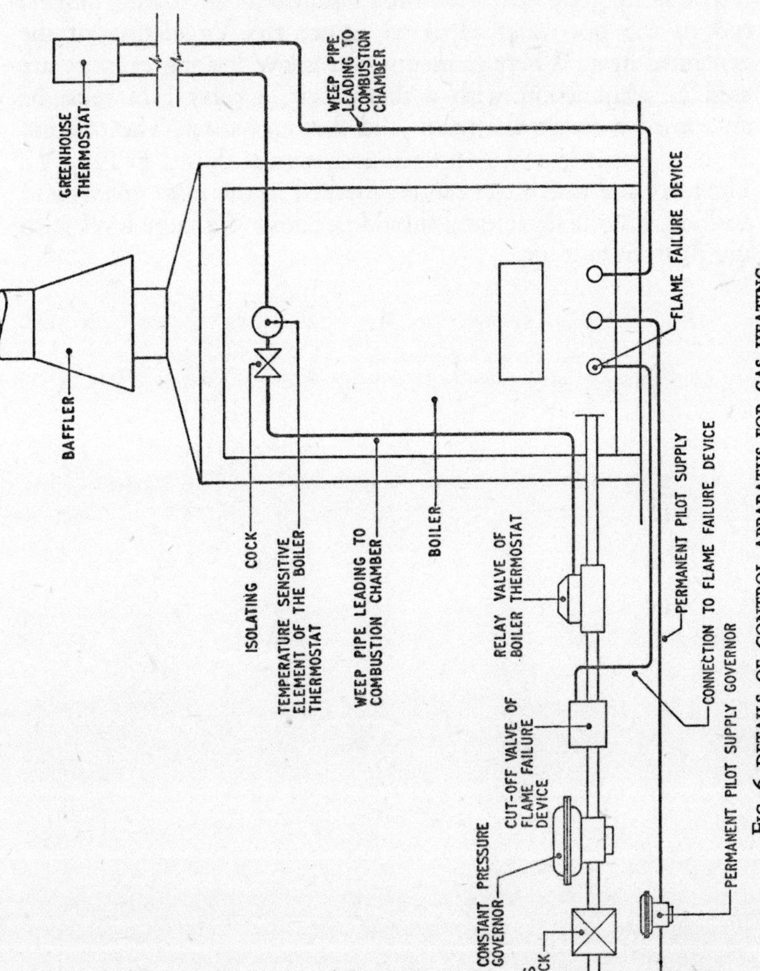

FIG. 6 DETAILS OF CONTROL APPARATUS FOR GAS HEATING.

subsequently reversed the process, I now use electricity as the main source for heating and gas as a stand-by.

The heating element should be installed at the lowest (boiler) end of the hot-water pipes to ensure free circulation of the generated heat. Where elements over 2 kW heating capacity are used in conjunction with a thermostat, a relay box must be interposed between the mains and the thermostat. The position of the element in my own heating system is shown in Plate VI. The relay and fuse boxes can be installed in the most convenient position, but the thermostat should be above the stage level with any form of heating.

4

HOUSE MANAGEMENT

GENERAL REMARKS

THE creation of good growing conditions, which will facilitate the assimilation process of our plants, must be uppermost in our endeavours. The beginner is often puzzled by the vastly differing interpretations of "good growing conditions" and well he might be, in view of the many different methods adopted by professionals and amateurs alike in the culture of orchids under glass. Looking back over the last twenty years, my own growing conditions have undergone a good many changes. "We live and learn," applies to orchid growing at least as much as to any other form of activity. There is no formula that could be singled out as the royal road to success and no finality in our quest for improvement of existing methods. I have seen excellent crops of flowers raised with a minimum of natural light in an atmosphere saturated with moisture, and equally good crops raised with leaves scorched and discoloured by the rays of the sun, with very little moisture in evidence.

Each method of growing has something to commend it, and since the production of flowers is our chief concern this must be the determining factor in our choice of growing methods—*i.e.*, house management. We may stick to one routine for years and consider it perfect, until we come face to face with developments that knock the bottom out of our conception of perfection. That is exactly what happened to me and which induced me to undertake a series of experiments on totally different lines to those hitherto pursued. Without wishing to disturb the peace of mind of satisfied growers, I will outline my new growing method for the benefit of the beginner and for those who have scope for improvement.

FALLACIES

As far back as I can remember it has been considered good culture to maintain a moist atmosphere in daytime and a dry one at night. How this concept came into being I do not know, but it has certainly become part of the "Bible" of orchid growing. In my opinion this is diametrically opposed to the assimilation process and rhythm of growth of the plants, inasmuch as the leaves absorb carbon dioxide from the atmospheric moisture—AT NIGHT; transpiring, through the effect of light and warmth—IN DAYTIME. The implications, therefore, are that the plants require moisture at night and a warm, dry atmosphere in daytime, to assist the rhythm of their organic functions. Furthermore, the leaves do not absorb, but give off, oxygen, which discounts the need for wide open ventilators at any time of the day or night.

PRACTICAL STEPS

Putting into effect this elementary understanding of the physiology of the plants, not without a certain amount of trepidation for "contravening" the time-honoured edicts of experts, I have carried out a series of experiments, first in one house and then in another. The result was a marked improvement in the texture and size of the leaves and new growths. Put into practice, the management in all three sections—*i.e.*, cattleya, cypripedium and odontoglossum—can be summed up as given in the following paragraphs.

ATMOSPHERIC MOISTURE

Some structures are, by their very nature, more moisture retentive than others. High brick walls and double glazing will automatically increase the moisture content in the atmosphere, unless extra ventilation is given as an antidote. Condensation on the glass, however, does not indicate the amount of moisture in the air—only the amount of moisture that has risen and condensed on the glass through the impact of the cooler outside temperature upon the warm air prevailing in the house. To accurately assess the moisture content of the atmosphere in relation to the temperature prevailing in the house at any given time a hygrometer must be used. Such an instrument could be useful to the novice by helping him to avoid extremes, but I have never possessed a humidimeter myself and would not concede more than an academic use for it at the hands of an experienced grower.

DAMPING DOWN

I am now treading on very controversial ground, but since the

PLATE XIII. Odontioda "Fred Bradley"

PLATE XIV. Cymbidium "Flycatcher" var. Wheatley, A.M.
(Photo: By courtesy of Wyld Court Orchids)

PLATE XV. Miltonia Seedlings on Vertical Staging

PLATE XVI. Vertical Staging in the Odontoglossum House

PLATE XVII. Corner in Odontoglossum House shown without "Clip-on" Potting Bench

PLATE XVIII. Cattleya Plant torn in two halves with minimum of root disturbance

PLATE XIX. Severed Odontoglossum Back-bulbs wrenched from leading portion

PLATE XX. "Clip-on" Potting Bench in position in the Odontoglossum House

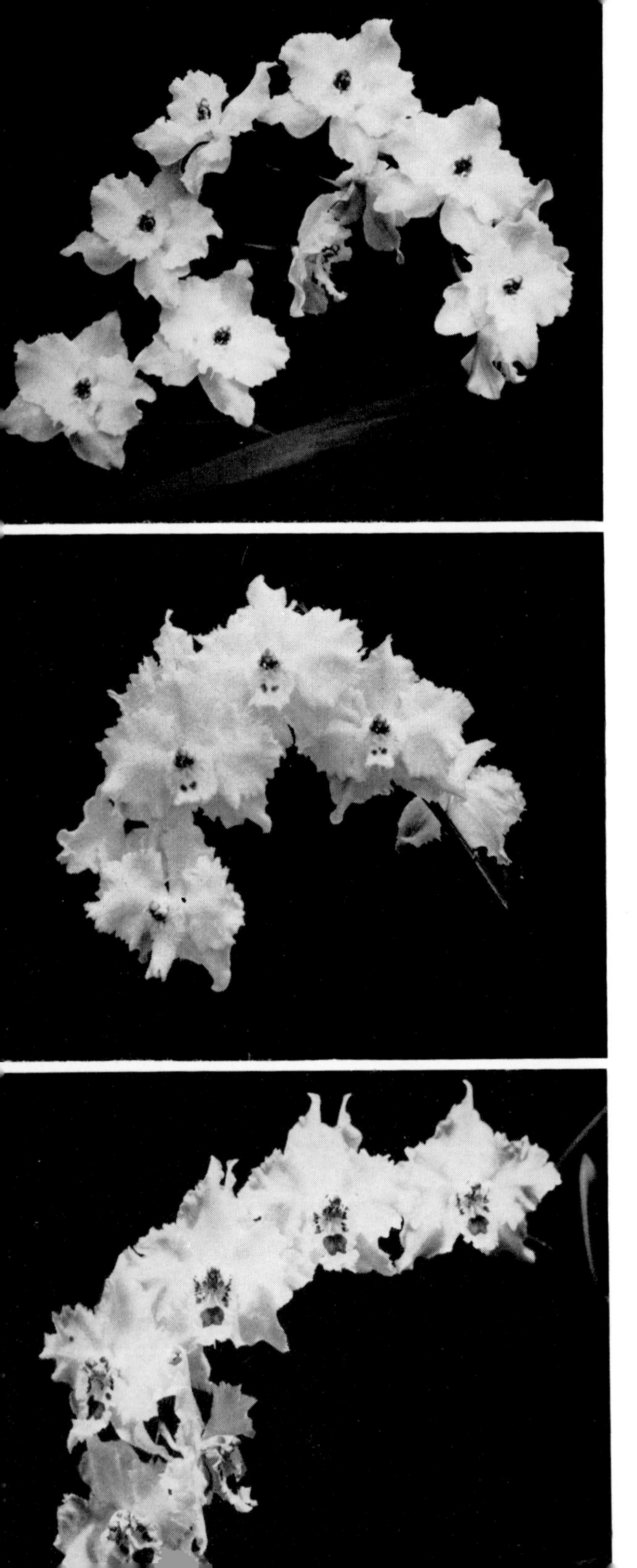

PLATE XXI
Odontoglossum
"Crispum Premier"

PLATE XXII
Another of the many
forms of Odontoglossum
"Crispum Premier"

PLATE XXIII
Odontoglossum
"Renton"

purpose of this book is to disclose my own method of culture, rather than to advocate methods and theories generally practised, I give my readers a description of the damping-down operation carried out in my own houses. One gallon of tap water per 100 square feet, applied after sunset through a rosed can to the floor only, represents the full extent of my damping-down operations. The reader should bear in mind, however, that the cement floor in my houses prevents the water from losing itself in the ground and must be absorbed by the atmosphere. The ventilators are closed before the damping-down operation and very little moisture can escape through a double-glazed roof. In the case of a single-glazed structure on a gravelly floor, up to four times as much water will be needed to obtain the same moisture content in the atmosphere. In daytime, no moisture is applied to any part of the house, apart from watering of the plants. Furthermore, I never spray my plants and have no moisture retentive stage. A lot of unnecessary work and attention is thus eliminated, for what I consider no help to the plants whatever. Much damping down in orchid houses is undertaken with a view to reducing the temperature in hot weather. In my own opinion, this is just wishful thinking, for any slight reduction of the temperature while plying the hose is only temporary and short-lived.

VENTILATION AND SHADING

With damping down thus reduced to a minimum, ventilation and shading must play their proper part to maintain the alternation of dry and damp conditions at their proper times. As already stated, the ventilators are closed at night before the damping-down operation. In the morning, immediately upon entering the houses, the ventilators are opened again an inch or two, according to the outside weather conditions. On very cold mornings it is advisable to delay the opening until the chill of an early frost has worn off and the inside temperature has risen sufficiently to prevent chilling of the plants. It is not only drier, but warmer conditions that are aimed at in daytime, otherwise the pores of the leaves will not open for the necessary evaporation and the normal functioning of the digestive or body-building cells is inhibited. Light itself plays a major part in the transformation of the carbon-dioxide-laden moisture absorbed during the period of darkness into starch and sugar, so essential to growth. Shading should therefore only be applied when it becomes necessary to prevent the inside temperature rising above a comfortable feel. In the case of "permanent" shading there is not much one can do to control the temperature in the house, but where blinds are in use they should be pulled over the house in good time to prevent the temperature running up to an uncomfortable level in hot weather.

TEMPERATURE

In the old days, when fuel was not such an expensive luxury, we used to divide orchids into Cool, Intermediate and Warm house plants, each house having its own recognized minimum and maximum temperatures when artificial heat was employed. Nowadays, most amateurs have to decide beforehand to which temperature their purses will stretch and draw the line accordingly. Necessity is said to be the mother of invention, and in the case of orchid culture, has taught us some useful, if not startling, lessons. We have thus found that strictly "cool house" subjects were doing better in a warm house temperature and vice versa and the above-mentioned definitions or divisions are no longer recognized and observed. If divisions have to be made, I prefer to consign plants to the cattleya, cypripedium, odontoglossum or cymbidium houses as being more representative of defined temperature ranges than the cool, intermediate or warm sections.

Odontoglossums, for instance, at one time were definitely considered "cool house," with a minimum temperature range between 45° and 50°, whereas success with this genus is stepped up with each degree of minimum temperature and at 60° minimum I have flowered most of my plants twice the same year. The temperatures given in this book refer to the Fahrenheit scale throughout. Cymbidiums, on the other hand, will flower more regularly in a temperature that is allowed to drop to 50°, or a few degrees lower at night. In the cypripedium section I would hate to see the temperature drop below 60° at any time, whilst the cattleyas will be quite happy with a minimum of 55°. The day temperatures should, if at all possible, rise at least 5° higher with artificial heat, and more if outside conditions permit. In countries with warmer climates, the temperatures given above will be exceeded considerably, with beneficial effect. Nothing is gained, however, with constantly overheated pipes, and better overall results are achieved by judicious selection of plants for which ideal conditions can be created.

Many amateurs have but one section to house their plants in, and in such cases shade is of equal importance with temperature in the selection of genus. Cattleyas would thus thrive in a cypripedium house temperature, but not with the amount of shading required by the latter. Miltonias will grow better with cypripediums, on account of the higher temperature, than with their near-relatives the odontoglossums. Both the miltonias and the odontoglossums would find the cattleya house temperature to their liking, but not the amount of light needed for cattleyas. The amateur will secure a far better return in terms of flower crops by a judicious selection of genera than by giving a free reign to his acquisitiveness and love for a "representative" collection. There are so many genera, each with its own wealth of choice, that it seems futile to fill a house with plants of incompatible cultural requirements, and this may well be the reason why so many amateurs fail to produce the goods at the shows.

In the chapter dealing with various genera I will attempt to make some suggestions for building up mixed collections, for the benefit of those amateurs with a special flair for variety.

WATERING

The flowering prospects of orchid plants depend in no small measure on correct watering. The compost in which they have been potted up may be poor or impoverished, the potting method slipshod and amateurish, attention casual and erratic—and still they flower! Some of these prolific flowerers never seem to have got a drop of water and yet three or four spikes are produced with clockwork regularity. Consider, for a moment, the same picture in reverse—plants on which attention has been lavished by a painstaking amateur in a house with all modern conveniences, and never a flower. The explanation, in nine out of ten cases must be sought in the frequency and method of watering. To know whether or not to water is the amateur's most difficult problem—and certainly the beginner's.

The most misleading factor in the domain of watering is the novice's experience with other pot plants, unless he has been growing cacti. Most of these plants have a network of very fine roots that penetrate the toughest compost throughout. New roots are constantly produced to absorb and pass on the moisture to the plant. Nearly all orchids have fleshy, and by comparison, thick roots which are in themselves veritable storehouses of moisture. Few roots are produced and then only at certain stages of the plant's development, which are not replaced once they are lost, to take care of its nutritional requirements. Some of these roots will not even penetrate the compost, trailing instead over it and over the edge of the pot, whilst others will hug the inside of the pot to make their way to the drainage hole and out of it if they can. What is the reason for this strange behaviour? The fact is that these fleshy roots do not search for moisture only, but for air as well, and they cannot live on moisture without air. This is best illustrated by the growth habit of epiphytic orchids growing on the branches of trees, with the whole length of the roots exposed to the air.

Under cultivation, orchid roots are tightly packed in a mixture of compost which expands when watered and by implication, displaces the air. When the compost dries out again, if it is allowed to, it contracts, readmitting air, which in turn keeps the compost healthy and porous. If this sequence of events is understood, the would-be grower is not likely to err again in the matter of watering his plants. He will simply let the compost dry out between waterings, thus keeping it in a healthy state and making available to the roots much-needed air.

It only remains for me to outline the best method of ascertaining the need for watering and when. "Instinct" is a valuable asset in this respect, but I usually back my impressions by lifting the plant that looks like needing a drink. If it feels light—and I mean light—it is immersed for a few seconds, up to a quarter from the pot rim. If it does not feel light, it goes unwatered until the next inspection—usually a week later. The reason for immersing only three-quarters of the pot is to keep the surface compost dry. This rule is occasionally waived by submersion, in order to keep the surface fresh. The sphagnum moss will not grow on the surface under these conditions, but the roots will grow into the compost in search of the moisture below. If the surface compost is kept constantly moist, the new roots tend to remain there and often perish before they have gained sufficient strength to penetrate the surface. This particularly applies to the tender-rooted odontoglossums and miltonias.

It is surprising how long some orchid genera can go before showing any signs of distress through underwatering. As already stated, the thick, fleshy roots of some pseudo-bulbless kinds, such as cypripediums, can make up for the absence of bulbs by their capacity to store moisture. Unlike the pseudo-bulbed epiphytes, they cannot show their need for watering by the shrivelling of their store bulbs. Periodic inspection by lifting the plants is in this case the only safe means of ascertaining their moisture requirements.

If a plant of any genus is kept constantly wet before the roots have penetrated the compost, the latter is bound to become sour and soggy in time and the roots will die. Such a plant may not flower again for several years, even if it survives such treatment. Repotting is imperative as soon as the discovery is made, paying particular attention to drainage and aeration.

Where large numbers of plants are grown, the watering-by-immersion method is impractical, as it would involve too much time and wide stages would further complicate the operation. In such cases, the water is usually applied with a rosed can, both on the surface and outside the pot. The latter, being porous, will pass moisture to the roots clinging to it inside, leaving the centre of the compost in a fairly dry state. This suits the cymbidiums in particular, as the great bulk of compost needed for adult plants remains wet for a long time after a thorough watering and there is the very real risk of it going sour if not discovered and rectified in time.

The frequency of watering varies considerably according to the method employed. During its period of growth an adult plant that has been watered by immersion can go from one to three weeks, according to season and prevailing weather conditions, and longer if the plant is of the resting kind, before needing further applications. If watered through a rosed can, the operation may have to be carried out daily, or every other day, and only an experienced grower should be entrusted with the task on this basis. Young seedlings, or plants in small pots, which dry out very quickly, should be attended to with the same frequency.

The uninitiated amateur is apt to draw the wrong conclusions when faced with the wet appearance of the plants at the nursery. The wet surface of the compost, the wet stage, and pots often covered with damp, lichenous growth, do not indicate or reflect the same conditions inside the pots, and many an amateur of my own acquaintance has gone home with the idea that he has been keeping his plants far too dry. Had he asked the usually obliging nurseryman to knock one of the plants out of the pot he would have come away with a somewhat different story. He might have found, as I did, that the compost was covered completely with thick, fleshy roots, but the plant itself, minus the pot, was so light as to suggest that it had never been watered at all. Thus the beginner is warned never to judge by appearances but to check up, whenever possible, before drawing conclusions.

5

POTTING MATERIALS

When I once asked the most successful orchid grower within my ken what materials he used to pot his plants in, he replied: "It does not matter what I use for potting compost, they [meaning his plants] all grow equally well whatever I use." That was undoubtedly the case with him, for he thoroughly understood how to use any kind of potting material and he was not the sort of man likely to slip up at watering times. I have not myself achieved such independence in the selection of potting materials and still consider the right choice of material of paramount importance for the well-being and progress of the plants. The grower who is away from home a great deal and has to allow longer intervals between waterings and repottings has to be more careful with the making up of his compost than the one who is in constant attendance. Again, the drainage does not assume the same importance in a country with a warm climate as it does in our country with an unpredictable, changeable climate, and the potting ingredients therefore must be chosen with a view to meeting these conditions.

OSMUNDA FIBRE

Fern root fibres are a universally recognized rooting medium and the staple diet of orchids under cultivation. Of these fern roots, osmunda is the most popular fibre in use for potting orchids and there are various reasons to account for this preference. It is readily available either in bales or cut up in convenient lengths in smaller quantities, affords good drainage and resists decomposition for a very long time owing to its coarseness and toughness. Three different kinds of osmunda fibre are available in this country—viz., the Japanese, American and Italian. Very little extraneous matter is found with the first two and they are tougher than the Italian osmunda. The latter, however, has the advantage of being considerably cheaper and no charge is made for the occasional ants' nests one comes across when pulling to pieces a bale of Italian osmunda, which should be cleaned and washed before being taken into the orchid house. Despite this handicap, I use Italian fibre in the potting mixture, but prefer to topdress the plants with either Japanese or American fibre, on account of its lasting quality.

ASPIDIUM AND POLYPODIUM FIBRE

During the last war polypodium fibre was collected from the mountainous regions of North Wales to take the place of osmunda, which was not then available. Aspidium fibre occurs in abundance in the Vosges and the Ardennes and is collected and used by French and Belgian growers, apparently in preference to osmunda fibre. Both the aspidium and polypodium root fibres make excellent potting material, but are more difficult and cumbersome to handle and you have to organize your own hunting expeditions to obtain this material.

SPHAGNUM MOSS

Once again I would like to quote a prominent grower of orchids, who had no use for sphagnum moss as a potting ingredient and who maintained that this medium was only being used for potting orchids on account of its cheapness. In the New World the growers manage very well without the use of fresh sphagnum moss in their potting compost and proof has thus been supplied in abundance that it is not an essential ingredient. This is borne out by my own experiments with cattleyas and genera, but not with the finer rooted genera such as odontoglossums and miltonias, which are doing better with a liberal proportion of live sphagnum moss. It has growth-promoting properties, very much in evidence with the seedlings of the finer rooted kinds, and retains moisture for longer periods than fibre only. Being cheap and readily available, therefore, nothing is gained by leaving out this useful ingredient.

OAK AND BEECH LEAVES

Dried oak or beech leaves, not to be confused with leafmould, and not collected from the road or verges where they can pick up injurious elements, constitute a useful addition to a fibre and moss mixture, resisting decomposition for a long time and thereby assisting aeration and drainage, eventually adding to the humus content of the compost. The leaves should be rubbed through a

PLATE XXIV

Laeliocattleya
"Fiesta"

PLATE XXV

Brassolaeliocattleya
"Ceylon Delight"

PLATE XXVI

Odontoglossum "Crispum Premier"

PLATE XXVII

Small group of Odontoglossums in flower. January 1957

PLATE XXVIII

Odontoglossum "Zeus"

½-inch mesh sieve and thoroughly mixed with the rest of the compost.

FIBROUS LOAM

Whilst the preceding elements are all that is needed for potting epiphytic orchids, such as cattleyas, miltonias, odontoglossums, oncidiums and vandas, the cymbidiums and the terrestrial cypripediums appreciate the addition of a proportion of good fibrous loam. Only best, lime-free fibrous loam should be used, pulled into small pieces and thoroughly mixed with the other ingredients used. The loam must be stored in a dry place and all small particles shaken out of it before use, thus only using the fibre with part of the loam adhering to it. It is safer to obtain the loam from an orchid nursery than to buy it indiscriminately from all and sundry. If it is not of a suitable kind, your plants would be better off without it.

TAN BARK

This material has not been used to any great extent in this country as a potting ingredient for orchids, although it has become very popular in some countries abroad. Experiments have been made with it here and there, but results have in some cases proved disappointing. Growing on trees and clinging to the bark, whence they absorb moisture and nutriment, it is difficult to divorce epiphytic orchids from their natural partiality to bark. If experiments with bark have failed, it is therefore safe to attribute our failures to indirect rather than direct causes. In my own experiments I have had failures and successes. The failures were all due to the bark disintegrating after a few months and after producing strong healthy roots and growths. The resulting powder prevented aeration in the compost and the toxic gases formed in consequence poisoned all but the surface roots. Further experiments with a fresh lot of tan bark, which had been washed and stored dry, produced totally different results, as the pieces of bark remained intact; having taken the precaution of thoroughly mixing the bark with the compost instead of pouring it into the pots around the old compost. If readers care to wash the bark obtained from the tanneries and store it in a dry place (not on the earth floor, as it will attract worms), a handy potting ingredient can thus be secured that will promote root growth at very little cost.

RECEPTACLES

Ordinary clay flower pots are used for the majority of orchids, preferably of the porous, hand-made type, as the smooth, machine-made pots, although pleasing to the eye while new, soon get covered with green lichenous growths. For the shallow-rooting kind of plants such as miltonias, or cattleyas with long, extending rhizomes, I prefer pans or three-quarter pots, to reduce the volume of compost which in such cases may easily become excessive. If the drainage hole in the pot is on the small side, turn the pot upside down and chip small pieces off the hole rim until a fair-size drainage hole is obtained. I do not favour pots or pans with multiple holes, sometimes called orchid pots. The roots have a habit of growing out of these holes and damage to the protruding roots is bound to occur sooner or later.

Teakwood baskets are appreciated by plants producing a number of aerial roots and, hung up on the roof at various levels, lend a touch of the exotic to the house. This exotic appearance is further enhanced by a few suitable plants tied to pieces of bark, with wads of fibre and moss worked in between the roots, fastened to purlin, uprights and glazing bars. Whether baskets or rafts, these must be easily removable for watering by immersion, as they soon get dried out. For small collections, this type of culture lends itself to all sorts of imaginative creations, especially if ferns and foliage plants are interspersed with the plants. It will give the enthusiastic amateur plenty of scope for whiling away his time, as watering will require almost daily inspection. Apart from the interest thus created, some plants with pendulous habits or drooping flower scapes can hardly be managed any other way.

CROCKS

The general practice in crocking up is to place a piece of earthenware crock over the drainage hole in order to retain the smaller pieces of crocks and compost. I prefer a cup-shaped piece of galvanized zinc crock, placed in an inverted position over the drainage hole. This will prevent the roots from growing out of the hole and bar the ingress of insects, which like to make their home among the crocks. If potsherds are used for drainage they should be arranged vertically, otherwise the flat pieces will merely form a false bottom above the drainage hole, thus defeating its own end. Brick rubble can be used to better advantage for this purpose, but I have found clinkers, broken up into convenient nut-shaped pieces, the most satisfactory and least troublesome material to prepare.

TOOLS

Light work can be had at the potting bench by securing the right sort of tools—at little expense. On quite a few occasions when I have been called upon to demonstrate proper potting technique to amateurs, I have found the task almost impossible owing to the complete absence of tools worthy of the name. More often than not my penknife and nail scissors had to be pressed into service in place of the broom-handle potting stick and the rusty old scissors that did not cut. Small wonder these good people thought they did a good day's work by repotting half a dozen plants!

A stainless steel pressed potting tool can be had for a couple of shillings, and many a stainless steel or chromium plated letter opener labelled "Souvenir" can be put to better use as a potting stick for orchids. The home-made variety of wooden potting sticks usually afford too much leverage, often culminating in too hard potting or broken pots. A pair of pinking shears with short blades for cutting up fibre, and a pair of curved scissors for trimming the compost surface, are the only other two essentials, taking for granted a sharp penknife for cutting off back-bulbs.

REPOTTING

The things I best remember from my early experiences at the potting bench are the heaps of broken pots, which in those days I looked upon as one of the "hazards" of the trade. Hard potting used to be the order of the day—at least that is how I was taught to pot. To lift a newly potted plant up by its leaves, without the pot falling away, was the hallmark of skilful potting. So in went that last tuft of fibre and moss and "bang" went the pot! In view of present-day prices for potting ingredients, it is as well we have grown out of that habit. In fact, we have become quite generous to the plants by allowing a little room inside the pot for the new roots. I certainly would not chance lifting any of my newly potted plants by their "ears."

POTTING BENCH

Those amateurs who possess a potting shed—usually the boiler house—can consider themselves very lucky, as it solves quite a few problems. Most amateurs have to use part of the stage or rig up a temporary potting bench inside the plant house. The latter is my choice, dictated by necessity—and the photograph Plate XX shows how I have improvised a "potting bench," which can be assembled or dismantled in a few seconds. This movable bench is shown assembled in the odontoglossum house, but can be fixed up in the cypripedium house should the prevailing temperature suggest such a course, for I am a great believer in comfort. A folding chair completes the equipment and this is used whenever a long potting session is anticipated. With the potting bench at a convenient height, these repotting sessions have become an enjoyable pastime, especially if the weather is cold and wet, which it usually is at weekends.

POTTING TECHNIQUE

The material for potting should be stored and roughly prepared outside, and only a sufficient quantity for immediate needs brought into the house to avoid the plants being smothered in dust and a variety of insects let loose among them. At the end of a potting session, another lot of material should be prepared and kept in the house to warm up in readiness for the next session. Sphagnum moss, which is usually wet and cold when first brought into the house, would chill the roots if used immediately. If kept inside the house, slugs and snails introduced in their embryos with fresh moss are bound to make their appearance.

Having made sure that the drainage hole in the pot is large enough, it should be covered with a perforated zinc crock in an inverted position, and crocks to about one-fifth of the pot's depth laid thereon. If a plant only needs "dropping on," the fresh compost is then gently worked round the front of the lead or last made-up pseudo-bulb. Root disturbance is generally looked upon as a necessary evil. Granted that some genera, notably cymbidiums and dendrobiums, resent root disturbance of any kind, the majority of orchids gain in vigour when relieved of old roots, shrivelled bulbs and spent compost. Whenever possible, therefore, I remove the back portion of a plant that is no longer capable of making a contribution to the leading or flowering growth. Such spent "passenger" bulbs can be a veritable drag and serve no useful purpose as an integral part of the plant. Potted up separately, it is often possible to coax new growths out of these severed back portions, which is a cheap way of increasing stock.

If the portion to be discarded is severed from the plant, before it is knocked out of the pot, by pushing the blade of a sharp knife through the rhizome, the live roots are less likely to be damaged by pressure and handling. The whole plant is then removed from the pot and each portion gripped firmly with the fingers of both hands and torn asunder. Most of the dead roots and spent compost will come away with the rear portion, and the cavity left in the centre of the growing portion will provide a convenient ingress for removing the rest of the spent compost still adhering to it without damaging the live roots. A little fresh compost is then inserted in the cavity provided and the plant pushed against the back of the pot, leaving space for the bulk of the fresh compost to be pressed against the live roots under the leading growth.

SURFACING

The rhizome of the leading growth will extend horizontally or upwards, but never downwards, calling for a surface layer of fresh compost to bring the base of the new growth level with the surface. Tease out some of the perished or lichenous compost from between the roots before resurfacing, to avoid the rhizome being buried in the new compost. In order to ensure maximum porosity of the surface compost, and not least for the sake of the appearance of the plants, the following method is recommended for resurfacing. Take a chunk of osmunda fibre and open it up with the fingers, but without tearing it apart. Insert wads of live sphagnum moss here and there, making a "sandwich" of fibre and moss. Trim the sandwich on all four sides and cut through the centre with the pinking shears. Join the two halves together side by side, with the cut surface uppermost, and you have the perfect surface, all fibres in a vertical position, ready to be wedged between the rhizome and pot edge. Use the potting tool to place the "sandwich" in position, pressing it down slightly inside the edge of the pot. Repeat the procedure until the whole of the surface is covered. With a little practice you will be able to trim the "sandwiches" into the correct sizes required for each position. Very little trimming of the covered surface is needed with this method and the surface will automatically slope down from the centre to the edge of the pot.

PITFALLS

Owing to one's natural reluctance of disturbing a plant in a thriving condition, it is often left in the same pot and compost until it shows signs of exhaustion or deterioration. When it is eventually dealt with it may take years of patient nursing to restore it to its former health and vigour. Far better to repot a plant at regular intervals, involving a minimum of disturbance, and while it is still in a condition to survive the action of the knife.

WHEN TO REPOT

As a general guide I recommend annual repotting for epiphytic orchids (using trees or rocks for their anchorage in their natural habitat) and biennially for geophytic or terrestrial orchids (growing on the ground). The root action of the epiphytic tribes is more confined to the season than that of the terrestrial tribes and is therefore a useful guide in determining the time of repotting of epiphytic orchids. The seasons of their natural habitats, however, do not coincide with our own and we therefore, whenever possible, choose the time when new root activity becomes apparent for repotting. This usually coincides with the formation of new growths, and whichever manifests itself first should be taken as an invitation for repotting. More precise hints will be given in the cultural directions for each genus dealt with in this book. Terrestrial orchids are most advantageously repotted as early in the spring as their flowering season permits—*i.e.,* after flowering.

It will be realized from the foregoing that it would be futile to use the calendar as a basis for potting operations. Furthermore, we are dealing mostly with hybrids of involved parentage, which bear little resemblance to the habits of the original species, and even if they did, the weather, at least in this country, is no respecter of seasons. Growth and root action being dependent to a high degree on light and warmth, however, repotting is best avoided from November to February, as far as this country is concerned. If, for specific purposes, repotting becomes necessary during the winter months, water should be withheld from such plants until signs of a revival can be discerned.

AFTER-POTTING TREATMENT

Newly potted plants should not be returned to their position of light on the staging, but grouped together in a heavily shaded place, preferably below the stage. The extra shade and warmth will contribute towards their re-establishment and prevent accidental watering. If the compost was moist at the time of potting, they will not need any further supplies of water for two or three weeks. An occasional dewing overhead when the inside temperature has exceeded the recognized minimum by about 5° F. will freshen the surface compost and encourage new growth. Until new root action has started, water should only be applied sparingly inside the pot rim. Some plants will get re-established quicker than others and should be returned to their original position on the stage, one by one, as progress warrants it. Watering of these plants should still be carried out with circumspection, as the increased bulk of compost will remain damp for longer periods, until the roots have penetrated it. If any doubt exists on the score of their progress or state of development, push the plants in question carefully out of the pot by holding them upside down, when the amount of root development can be ascertained, replacing the pot carefully after examination, without disturbing either compost or crocks.

The plants that appear to have come to a standstill, not to be confused with those that have undergone their natural period of rest, are very often left to "sulk" for months on end in the same pot and compost. Provided other conditions are somewhere near the mark, the fault must be looked for inside the pot. The compost may be unsuitable, potting too hard; the compost may have "balled up" into a solid mass preventing aeration, or turned sour. Hardly noticeable beginnings of a combination of these troubles may have killed the old roots and inhibited the formation of new ones. Sometimes the cause of the trouble is not discernible at all, but the plant may romp away when potted up in a fresh lot of compost. In any case, nothing is gained by leaving a plant to "sulk."

Overpotting is another likely source of trouble—and a frequent one at that. If a plant is repotted annually, then overpotting is not likely to occur. It is when the amateur tries to fix the plant up for the next two or three years that overpotting takes place. Before the elapse of this period the compost will have spent itself and either have gone solid or sour; in either case preventing aeration of the roots. If it has survived these vicissitudes, the plant has to be dealt with far more drastically at the potting bench than usual by the removal of two or three years' growth and most of the old compost.

6

MANURING

THIS chapter is included in the book more in the nature of a warning than encouragement to the amateur who may be thinking of resorting to manurial aids in order to secure a bigger, or better, crop of flowers from his orchids. Manures of any kind, whether organic or synthetic, are no substitute for good growing conditions as far as orchids are concerned. Orchids do not respond to manurial aids in the same way as most other plants do, and even the exceptions are limited to the use of weak, or slow-acting, organic manures. Examples of these exceptions are calanthe, for which weak cow manure is recommended during the growing season, cymbidiums and zygopetalums, which gain in vigour by the addition of hoof and horn meal.

Manurial stimulants applied to other orchids will in most cases result in upsetting the balance between the growth and flowering hormones, favouring the former at the expense of the latter. Experiments carried out with some medium-sized cattleyas, for instance, produced five, six, and in one case even eight new growths, by incorporating $\frac{1}{20}$th part of hop manure (to which has been added superphosphate of lime) in the compost. The same experiment carried out with odontoglossums caused some plants to break out in three or four places, but all of them failed to flower. The flowers obtained from the cattleyas were smaller and of a weaker texture and they did not in consequence last more than a few days. Similar results were obtained from the cypripediums, but they in addition, lost their roots and had to be rescued from the experimental compost to save the plants.

Experiments carried out with organic as well as synthetic fertilizers, if they did not kill the plants, all more or less culminated in accelerated but weakened "floppy" growths, smaller flowers of poor texture and premature decomposition of the compost. The last-mentioned development was the most serious, as the rotting compost formed a solid mass, preventing any form of root aeration and, where not dealt with in time, led to the destruction of the roots by the resultant toxic gases. No good purpose can be served by listing the details of these experiments which clearly prove that, from the point of view of the amateur, manuring of orchids is not a practical proposition. The nurseryman, on the other hand, may not be so much concerned with the production of flowers as with a quick method of increasing his stock, in which case there is something to be gained from a deeper study of this problem.

The most valuable lesson I have derived from my experiments with manurial aids is the knowledge that strong, sturdy and luscious growths on orchids are not to be gained by root feed of any kind, but by assisting the biological functions of the plants—in other words, by establishing a correct balance between light, warmth and atmospheric moisture, both in daytime and during the hours of darkness. This is a field which offers much scope for exploration, as well as the promise of glittering prizes: see page 61.

7

PESTS AND DISEASES

FORTUNATELY for the hobbyist, orchids are highly resistant to diseases, and where they are met with it is usually a constitutionally weakened plant that is involved. Cleanliness in orchid houses is something that should be taken for granted and, combined with the maintenance of good, healthy growing conditions, is the best insulation against pests and diseases. No nurseryman in this country will supply infected plants, and imported plants should be kept in isolation for a week or two before being staged among the other plants. Non-orchidaceous plants grown among orchids are often the main attraction for pests, and these sometimes develop a liking for the latter. The old adage "Prevention is better than cure," if acted upon, will prevent any serious outbreak of disease or infestation of plants.

FUMIGATION

Fumigation is probably the oldest method of pest control in glasshouses. Much progress has been made in this field since the days when nicotine auto-shreds were the only known fumigant. Special preparations are now available to deal effectively with the most insidious and persistent of pests. Up to the present time, however, I have not come across a preparation that is effective for all pests but, judging by the progress already made, it is only a matter of time for the scientists working to this end to evolve a universal remedy.

Since the advent of DDT, thrips are no longer the dreaded pest they used to be, and one fumigation with DDT smoke generators, used in accordance with the makers' instructions, will not only destroy this pest but prevent their recurrence for many months. DDT fumigations are also effective for most other insects, including scale and woodlice, but will not dispose of red spider. For this pest, azobenzine and chlorocide fumigants should be used in two applications, at six to eight days' interval.

Effective control by fumigation, however, can be achieved

only if a temperature of 70° F. or over can be maintained for at least four hours and if the house to be fumigated can be made smoke-tight. Broken panes of glass must first be replaced and gaps around doors and ventilators must be blocked up to prevent the smoke from escaping. A mild, windless day should be chosen for this operation and, if at all possible, the glass roof should be covered with canvas or other suitable material. The house should not be re-entered the same day, but left shut until the following morning. All plants in need of watering must be watered beforehand, but the foliage kept dry, whilst the paths should be soaked to create a moist atmosphere, which increases the effectiveness of the fumigation.

SPRAYING

Spraying with a fine nozzle, to produce a mist-like dew, is more effective in cases where the house cannot be made smoke-tight, or in unsuitable weather when the required high temperature cannot be maintained. Here again DDT wettable powder or liquid emulsions mixed to the makers' prescribed strength will dispose of most pests. For the control of red spider, the comparatively new Chlorocide wettable powder has a lasting effect, requiring one thorough spraying only. Another recent introduction for combating red spider is the aerosol jet atomizer, which is probably the most convenient remedy in use. It is supplied in small canisters, with a spring-loaded knob on top, which emits a continuous jet of fine, mist-like spray when depressed. It is particularly suitable for dealing with isolated cases, when a few seconds' spraying is sufficient to cover from one to half a dozen plants. When a larger number of plants have to be treated, direct the jet into the air space above the plants, working your way towards the door away from the treated area. Unlike DDT emulsions or Chlorocide, aerosol does not leave behind unsightly white blotches on leaves, glass and stage after treatment. It does not have to be mixed with water and is ready for instant use when and as required.

With slugs, snails and woodlice, one has to be constantly on the look-out and no single application of any remedy, no matter how effective it may be, will render the house immune for any length of time. As soon as one lot has been disposed of by spraying with DDT walls, paths and the floor below the stages, another lot of these pests find their way into the house, probably in their embryos by way of the new compost, the moss being no doubt the chief culprit.

Except for stretching muslin or gauze across the open ventilators, there is not much one can do about the aerial raiders. A whole trail of devastation can result from chasing these intruders, the larger ones, notably the bumble and honey bees and bluebottles, often being responsible for the fertilization and collapse of a whole string of flowers. The flies are usually taken care of by the spiders, whose webs I never disturb on purpose, and for the sake of their preservation, I do not fumigate.

DISEASES

The most pernicious of diseases in connection with orchids is that caused by virus, fortunately very rare in this country. Fungus diseases are more prevalent and have their origin in some cultural lapse or misunderstanding of a plant's requirements. For this reason, this trouble is more often met with in mixed collections than among genera grown separately by themselves. For the sake of the collection, a virus infected plant should be burnt, whereas removal of parts affected by fungus may give the plant another chance. The cause of fungus attacks must be investigated, however, and remedial measures taken to prevent the trouble from spreading, or recurring. Fungus only thrives in damp, close conditions and we should not, therefore, have far to look for the cause of the trouble. It manifests itself in many different ways, damping-off being most frequently encountered. Here, drips, or careless watering, combined with insufficient heat or lack of fresh air, are the most likely causes. With cypripediums, it shows as bud-rot; with odontoglossums and miltonias the central leaf or leaves present an oily appearance, whilst in the case of cymbidiums the base of the bulb goes soft. Fungus can also account for the wet mould and oily patches on odontoglossum or miltonia leaves. Having encountered this trouble myself a few years ago among the odontoglossums, before they were housed separately, my advice is—ventilate freely and refrain from damping down in daytime, as well as from spraying the leaves, taking care that the day, and night, temperatures are kept up to their recognized minimum—a few degrees higher in daytime.

8

CHRISTOPHER BRANCH

THE name of Christopher Branch spells magic among the orchid growers, amateurs and professionals alike, who are "in the know" about the achievements of this wizard of orchid culture. I make no apologies for using the word "wizard" in connection with this man, who had everyone flabbergasted at the sight of his handiwork. This book would not be complete without a testimony and tribute to the finest orchid grower within my ken, who has wrenched many a secret from Nature's veiled treasury and to whom I owe a great debt for his example and encouragement.

Who sold flowers from odontoglossum plants taken from a community pot two years previously? Who else but Christopher Branch! Who increased a stock of two cypripedium Clair de Lune to thirty-five plants in four years? Christopher Branch! Who grew two successive flowers from the same growth of cypripediums? Indeed, who else but Christopher Branch! This catalogue of unique achievements could be carried into the field of cattleyas, cymbidiums and any other orchid entrusted to the care of Christopher Branch.

If you fellow orchidists think this is fantastic, you had better hold your breath and listen to what I have seen in the man's odontoglossum house! I do not know the exact number, but a conservative estimate would put it at 750 plants. Each plant carried from two to four bulbs, mostly three and not one of these bulbs showed the slightest sign of shrivelling! On the contrary, I had never before seen such fat, shining bulbs that looked like having been polished into the bargain. You never saw two bulbs of the same size on a plant, for each successive bulb was doubled, trebled and, in some cases quadrupled! But the most amazing sight of all was a tiny seedling bulb behind a monster bulb of some 4 inches in height and nearly as wide, carrying a long, thick flower spike. When propagating from a back-bulb one does not normally expect the first growth to equal the size of the parent bulb. Christopher Branch grew a larger one which, as often as not, flowered. A sickly plant put in his care was usually returned with a flower spike a few months later.

Quite naturally, you want to know the secret behind such astounding successes. According to Christopher Branch himself, the reason is plain common sense. This, to most people who have, like myself, seen his plants and probed his methods as far as possible, sounds terribly inadequate. Nobody has, to my knowledge, been able to get anywhere near the classic standard of Orchid culture set by this horticultural genius. It appeared to me that he had reversed every accepted practice known in Orchid culture and thereby hit on a growing method which is far more conducive to plant development than anything I have previously, or since, chanced across.

Let me, first of all, point out that Christopher Branch has never read a book on orchid culture. He therefore never saddled himself with any set notion on how orchids should be grown and consequently never copied anybody's mistakes. He started from "scratch" and was thus able to evolve his own methods of culture which were based solely on his own observations of the plants in his care. Christopher Branch has no use for fertilizers or artificial aids of any kind and considers them unnecessary and undesirable. Earlier, when I first came face to face with these astounding achievements, I had my doubts on this score, but I am now satisfied that such results could not be achieved through root-feed.

The first thing that struck any visitor to his odontoglossum, or any other house, was the complete absence of any trace of moisture. There was no moisture staging and the plants stood on an open slatted stage. The ground underneath was dry and so was the path between the stages. The only damping down, if it can be called such, was at night after shutting the ventilators. This was done with a rosed watercan, walking up and down the path with it once only. Obviously, therefore, the only moisture present in the house was found at night. Without going into, or bothering about, the photosynthetic ritual of the plants, Christopher Branch instinctively knew what they wanted and when they wanted it!

You will have noticed that I have written in the past tense, as the wizard of orchids is, unfortunately, crippled with rheumatoid arthritis and unable to take an active part in orchid culture any more. How is it possible, you may ask, that a man with such outstanding achievements, which could have earned a fortune for any orchid nursery, is so little known outside a comparatively small circle? To find the answer to this question, it is necessary to study the man's background as well as his character. My appreciation of his characteristics, however, is greater than my ability to put them into words. Whatever I may have to say about him is doing but scant justice to a genius.

Picture for yourselves a quiet, unassuming, unobtrusive, retiring sort of a man, whose only ambition in life, apart from bringing up a family, was growing orchids. It did not matter to him who he grew them for or what he got for it, as long as he was allowed to do things his own way, in his own time, without interference from any quarter. He loved orchids, whether they belonged to him or someone else, and they filled his mind to the exclusion of any thoughts of exploiting his achievements. His deafness had a lot to do with his retiring ways and the company of other humans was something to be shunned, certainly not cultivated. Using his own words, "When you are deaf, people think you are a damn fool." Being deaf myself, I have a great deal of sympathy for this statement, although it does not affect me in the same way and to the extent it influenced him. He was happier working as the grower of private collections than he was working alongside other growers in a nursery. The suspicion his outstanding cultural skill earned him at the hands of his colleagues was too much for a sensitive man like Christopher Branch to jog along with for any length of time. Everybody who worked with him seemed to look for that non-existent bottle of magic, which caused a lot of unnecessary resentment, and, having no personal ambitions, the man preferred to relinquish his employment rather than work in an unhappy atmosphere.

That is the picture, as I see it—if not a sorry tale—of a genius who is now lost to the cause of orchid growing, but the name of Christopher Branch will always occupy first place in the admiration of those who saw his handiwork.

9

GENERA

TO GIVE a comprehensive description with cultural advice on all genera of the vast orchid family, with its thousands of known species and many more thousands of hybrids, lies beyond the confines of any single book and the purpose of orchid growing as a hobby. The hobbyist, with one or two glasshouses to contain his collection, can at the most hope to collect a few of the better-known genera, comprising both species and hybrids, which will offer him an inexhaustible choice of varieties. His main purpose being the cultivation of plants that will provide him with a good show of flowers, especially during the dreary winter months, he will not be so much concerned with rare species or such plants that will fill his restricted space with vegetation. The trade orchid growers have recognized this preference and concentrated their hybridization programmes upon genera of easy culture and generous flowering habit. Once their general culture is understood, the hobbyist will have acquired sufficient knowledge to guide him in the selection of more ambitious subjects of differing growing habits and requirements.

The genera selected in this book are those which offer the greatest scope and promise and with which the author has had personal growing experience. For a more comprehensive treatise on genera, *Orchids, Their Description and Cultivation,* by Charles H. Curtis, published by Putnam, should be consulted.

SPECIES AND HYBRIDS

Species are the type from which the hybrids have been derived by crossing with other species or hybrids thereof. Not all species have been imported from their countries of origin, for as demand exceeded supply, the growers have either "selfed" some species (pollen applied to the stigmatic plate on the same plant) or crossed two plants of the same species, in order to make good the deficiency. In a never-ending quest to improve size and colour of the flowers, to add vigour to some and prolong the flowering

PLATE XXIX
Odontonia
"Avrania," var.
Lyoth Sultan

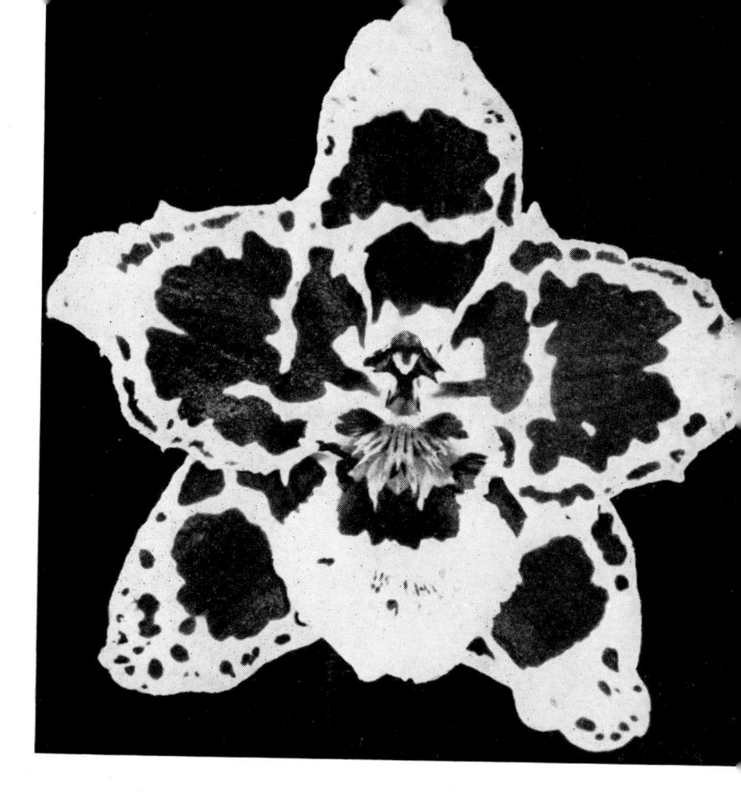

PLATE XXX. Odontonia "Mena," Whitton var.

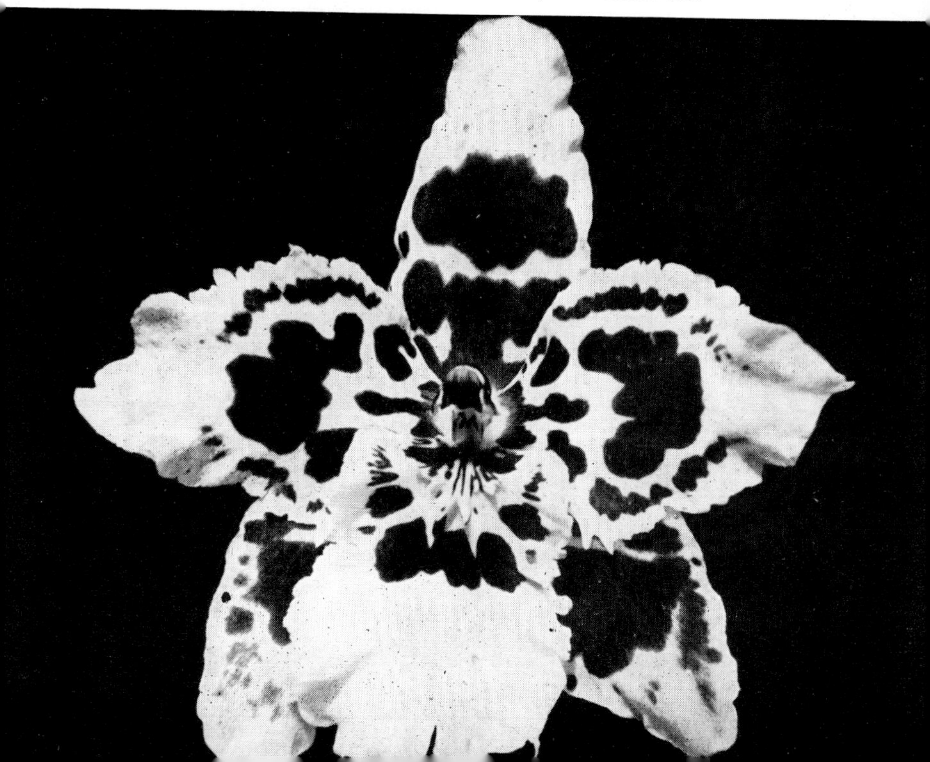

PLATE XXXI
Odontioda "Refulcis"

PLATE XXXII
Odontoglossum "Welland"

PLATE XXXIII
Vuylstekeara "Estelle Jewel,"
var. Maori

season of others, to transfer desirable features from one to another, species and their resultant hybrids have been crossed and inter-crossed with the result that the modern hybrids often bear little resemblance to their original parents. Some of the species, once popular, have gradually disappeared from our collections, to make room for their more striking or impressive offshoots. But not all species have been eclipsed by their progeny. There are some that have refused to hybridize and others that can still hold their own among our modern hybrids and often excite more interest by virtue of their unique flower formation, their mimicry of the animal and insect worlds, or of their exquisite scent. Thus most of our collections will continue to be composed of both species and hybrids, bringing interest and joy into the pursuit of our hobby all the year round.

As the list of interesting species given in some of the genera could be extended considerably, it is quite impossible to give a representative list of hybrids. Thousands of hybrids have been registered in Sanders' Lists of Registrations and many more crosses have been made, which some growers have not bothered to register, or which have not been found worthy of registration. It must be realized also that each cross produces many varieties of differing shapes, sizes and colours, often hardly bearing any resemblance to one another. An abridged list of hybrids would only be an arbitrary one and of little use to the enquirer, who cannot do better than to visit an orchid nursery and make his own selection according to taste and purse.

10

ODONTOGLOSSUM

HERE surely we have a genus that, if not created specially for the convenience and delight of the amateur orchid grower, will gladden the heart of every lover of floral beauties. The graceful, arching sprays of flowers, often 3 feet long and coming from diminutive plants in 3-inch pots or thereabouts, never fail to compel the admiration of all comers, with rows of evenly spaced out delicate blooms, ranging from a chaste white to a dark purple or maroon, or with intermingling colours bordering on the bizarre. Such are the beauty and unsurpassable qualities of the odontoglossum.

I have given pride of place to this tribe not only because the Creator has excelled Himself by adorning His flora with the odontoglossum's outstanding beauty, but because He has also seen fit to endow it with prolific flowering potentialities. Bearing in mind the exceptionally long flowering season, lasting from September to the following July, and the modest amount of space required by the plants, the odontoglossum should be first favourite among amateur orchid growers.

It is therefore all the more deplorable that odontoglossums have become the Cinderella of most collections, having been tainted with the notion that they are difficult to flower. Given a reasonable chance, odontoglossums will flower with clockwork regularity—in fact, the only drawback under good cultivation is that they try to flower too often. In most cases where success with odontoglossums has eluded the grower, they have been treated as something like semi-aquatics under cool-house conditions. In the attempt to keep the temperature down to "cool house" level in warm weather, the atmosphere in the odontoglossum house has too often been overcharged with moisture, which is one of the worst things that can happen to the plants. I utterly refute the notion that odontoglossums are "cool-house" orchids, at least as far as our home-raised hybrids are concerned. Neither the geographical position (*i.e.*, proximity to industrial areas) nor the geological formation of the ground have anything to do with the success of these plants.

The foundations for our notions of odontoglossum culture have been laid many years ago, when imported species and primary hybrids formed the bulk of collections. In their natural habitat odontoglossums grow at high altitudes, often at elevations of 10,000 feet. Transplanted into totally different climatic conditions, every effort had to be made to create conditions akin to those prevailing in their natural state—*i.e.*, on high mountain ranges. The affinity of primary hybrids does not vary much from their progenitors or species. For many years, odontoglossums were grown very successfully in this country and constituted the bulk of exhibits at orchid shows. As the years went by, mainly home-raised plants which had become thoroughly acclimatized to artificial culture were used for hybridizing, until a totally new race of plants was evolved which would not flourish in the climatic conditions in which their ancestors revelled. This process—call it the evolution of the odontoglossum—has been going on steadily and imperceptibly for half a century, and the time has come to face the fact that the early cultural instructions handed down to us by successive writers no longer apply. Judging by the success achieved with odontoglossums by some of the contemporary growers, the change in the situation has already been realized by them and acted upon.

HOUSING

Where a house can be devoted exclusively for the cultivation of odontoglossums, near-ideal conditions can be created for these plants by providing a free circulation of air and ample shading. A lean-to house facing north is ideally suited for these shade-loving plants and such a structure could not be put to better use. Next in the order of suitability is a span-roof house with high brick walls—*i.e.*, without side lights. If side lights are present it is a simple matter to block these up with a lining of hardwood. It is not only a matter of shutting out too much light, but primarily one of insulating the house against outside atmospheric conditions, and for this reason I advocate lining of the roof with Windolite or Polythene as well. Coupled with ample shading on the roof, the owner will thus be able to exercise a certain amount of control over the inside atmospheric conditions without overheating the pipes during cold spells. Attention must of course be paid to doors and ventilators to ensure close fitting and to avoid loss of heat and atmospheric moisture when closed. If such a house receives shading by overhanging branches of a near-by tree, the owner will get things pretty well his own way without much effort. However, trees do not often grow that way and they certainly did not in my garden.

SHADING

As most growers will have to manage without a tree handy enough to do the job for them, blinds will have to be provided to keep strong sunlight away from the roof glass, otherwise the inside temperature will get out of control. "Permanent" shading by painting over the roof glass, if applied thick enough, will provide the necessary shade but do little to keep the temperature within bounds during hot spells. Pinolium blinds provide the best means of shading for an odontoglossum house. Lath blinds require an additional coat of paint on the roof glass facing south. Remember, the best provisions will come to nought without adequate shading. Reduce the amount of shading gradually, from October onwards, until the blinds can be taken off altogether.

TEMPERATURE

Most of the inmates of the odontoglossum house will be hybrids raised from acclimatized parents and the temperature should therefore be adjusted to suit them. A minimum night temperature of 55° F., with a few degrees less during very cold spells, and a day temperature of 60° F. or over, will keep the plants growing. A few degrees less will not hurt the plants but will slow down their rate of growth, which is preferable to driving the fires. Species or primary hybrids can manage on considerably less heat, in fact are better for it, and if they are arranged around the ventilators, or outside door, the conditions should suit them. Whilst the above temperature ranges apply for the greater part of the year in this country, when fire heat has to be provided, the warm summer weather will often drive the day temperature up into the eighties. No harm will come to the plants, provided sufficient ventilation is given to avoid a close, stuffy atmosphere. The night temperature will be around 60° F., and if the outside temperature is not likely to drop to that level, close the ventilators in the evening and damp the floor down, including the path.

VENTILATION AND ATMOSPHERIC MOISTURE

Whilst odontoglossums, like all other orchids in their natural habitat, receive fresh air all the time, the supply of atmospheric moisture at high altitudes is restricted mainly to the hours of darkness. Growing them under glass practically at sea level, these conditions have to be artificially created. In our climate, dry hot days will not necessarily be followed by damp nights, and damp nights are often too cold to take advantage of. That is why ventilation and atmospheric moisture are so closely bound up together as to be inseparable from a cultural standpoint.

Open the ventilators an inch or two in the morning, as soon as the required temperature has been reached in the house, whatever the weather conditions outside. This is necessary to replace the moisture-charged atmosphere with fresh air. Keep at least a crack open all day, even in cold weather, more if the weather is mild or warm. Close the vents again in the evening before the sun has set, when the weather is hot and dry and when artificial heat has to be used. Damp down the floor under the stages, as well as the path, which can be made the last operation before retiring. When the nights are damp and cool there is no need to close the ventilators and damping down should be omitted, as sufficient atmospheric moisture will find its way into the house through the ventilators. Under the conditions thus created the absorption of moisture, followed by transpiration by the leaves, will take a natural course, to which your odontoglossums cannot fail to respond.

ENCOURAGING FLOWERING

Having come across a number of cases where odontoglossums have been grown into strong plants with large, fat pseudo-bulbs, which persistently refused to flower, I think it might help others with similar problems to counteract such disconcerting habits of their plants, by relating my own experience.

In actual fact, my own case is just the opposite, inasmuch as many of my plants persistently showed spike before the bulbs had even started to make up, or soon after. With this handicap, the bulbs cannot be expected to grow to, or near, their maximum size and neither do the resultant flower spikes. If the spikes are allowed to develop under these conditions, weakened plants will result, which may require a couple of years or more before they can regain flowering status.

According to general practice, plants approaching flowering size are given more light in order to ripen off the growths and encourage the formation of flower spikes. It was not, however, until I thought of reversing this process that I managed to induce flowering of my plants at their correct stage of development. This entailed admitting more light to the plants at an earlier stage, thus favouring plant growth at the expense of flower development.

Having thus succeeded in retarding the production of flower spikes, by increasing the light volume, it can be safely assumed that shy flowerers can be induced to initiate flower development by decreasing the volume of light through shading. At what stage this should be done cannot be stated yet with any degree of accuracy. This is a matter for experimentation under laboratory conditions, which is beyond the writer's scope. Suffice it to say for the present that a three-quarters made-up bulb not showing any intention of flowering, has never subsequently failed to do so, in the writer's experience, when subjected to a period of comparative darkness.

Once the flower spike has emerged from the sheath or bract, it does not seem to matter whether the plant itself is given short-day or long-day conditions. The spike, growing upwards, helps itself to the extra light needed for its further development. The same responses have been noticed in the cattleya section and no doubt other genera are subject to the same laws governing plant development, to varying extent.

In view of the observations made, particularly in the odontoglossum house, there is now no doubt in my mind that darkness favours the development of the hypothetical flowering hormones, whereas light encourages the growth hormones. When the two are well-balanced, growth and the production of flowers will go hand in hand, but where one set of conditions preponderates, corrective measures may have to be taken to bring about the desired results. Here, as elsewhere, observation of the plants is the safest guide.

POTTING MATERIALS AND REPOTTING

Odontoglossums have fine, tender roots with little penetrating power and the only exceptions are found in one or two species. To cram the compost hard into the pot will prevent aeration so essential to these roots and impede the capillary function of the compost itself, no matter how well balanced this may be. Fairly loose potting is required, and obtained by working the compost gently between the roots and filling all empty spaces. This will ensure a better distribution of the roots and uniform wetting of the compost when watering. The surface layer of the compost, if applied in the manner described in an earlier chapter, will hold the plant firm and steady and prevent loose particles of the compost being washed out of the pot.

The compost should be made up of equal parts of osmunda fibre and sphagnum moss, both chopped up finely and thoroughly mixed. Add to this about one-fifteenth in bulk of dried oak leaves, rubbed through a sieve, or one-tenth of acid-free tan bark, well mixed with the bulk of the compost. The surface layer of compost should consist only of fibre and moss.

Repotting is best done annually, or at least once every second year. Remove all back-bulbs in excess of three behind the lead, together with the roots and compost adhering to them. Carefully tease out any firmed-up chunks of compost from the main stock of the plant and replace with new compost. Do not disturb the compost directly under the last made-up bulb, where most of the new roots are concentrated. Proceed as described in "Potting Technique" (p. 52).

WATERING OF ODONTOGLOSSUMS

Although watering of orchids in general has already been dealt with earlier on in this book, this subject is of particular importance where odontoglossums are concerned and does not, therefore, brook any misunderstanding. One untimely application of water, can, under certain circumstances, undo all the good done to a particular plant for months past. During warm, bright spells of weather, when the compost dries out fairly quickly, this is not likely to happen. It is during spells of prolonged cold weather that the danger arises, especially where newly potted plants are concerned. Such plants, by virtue of the increased bulk of compost, which has not been penetrated by new roots as yet, remain wet for a very long time. Should they receive water, by accident or design, before the compost has dried out, the new roots are likely to die and the compost to turn sour, with the result that the new growth will not develop satisfactorily.

Nothing of this sort is likely to happen if the compost is allowed to dry out before watering. Lift each plant at fairly regular intervals and only water those that feel light. Place the larger plants together in one group; the smaller in another; the seedlings in a third; and keep the newly potted plants separate to facilitate inspection. The large plants and the newly potted ones will require a weekly inspection at the most and only a few may be found in need of watering. The smaller plants and the seedlings should be inspected twice a week, but only watered where necessary. If the method of watering suggested earlier on—*i.e.*, watering by immersion (not submersion) up to three-quarters of the pot's depth—is carried out whenever the compost has dried out, no mistakes are likely to occur in this respect.

Odontoglossum species enjoy a period of rest after flowering, which coincides with the dry season in their country of origin. The length of their resting season varies from species to species, culminating in approximately three months' dormancy inherent in the odontoglossum grande. During such periods of inactivity only scant supplies of water at longer than usual intervals should be administered, to keep the compost fresh and prevent excessive shrivelling of the bulbs. The moment new breaks appear, normal watering should be resumed. These periods of rest, of whatever duration, are not a constitutional part of the biological functions of the plant, but merely a condition imposed by prolonged drought. Under cultivation, a species may forgo its period of rest altogether.

The modern hybrid, being the result of crossing a number of parents of different origin, and therefore different habits, has no discernible period of rest. Watering should therefore be carried on as usual after flowering. For some weeks after it has been relieved of its flower spike a hybrid odontoglossum will require less frequent applications of water than it did when in full growth, as indicated by the compost remaining moist for longer periods.

Shrivelling of the bulbs is not necessarily an indication that more frequent watering is needed—the reverse may be the case. Allow such plants to dry out in the usual way and then give them a good soaking by submersion. If the leading bulb does not plump up soon after this extra helping, knock the plant out of the pot and examine both roots and compost. Repot in fresh compost if necessary.

PLATE XXXIV. Odontoglossum "Porthos," "Zebrina" var.

PLATE XXXV. Miltonia "Beethoven," var. Symphony

PLATE XXXVI
Cymbidium "Prince Charle
var. Regal

Photos: By courtesy of Messrs. Black & Flory Ltd.

PLATE XXXVII. Cymbidium "Balkis," var. Solent Queen

PLATE XXXVIII

Cypripedium
"Rosy Dawn"

PLATE XXXIX

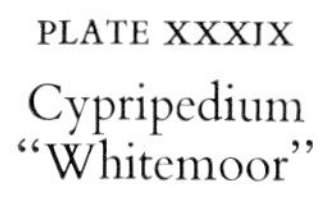

Cypripedium
"Whitemoor"

PLATE XL

Cypripedium
"Bruno," var. Model

PLATE XLI

Cypripedium
"Gwyneth"

PLATE XLII

Cypripedium
"Fulmar" × Spring Verdu

PLATE XLIII

Cypripedium
"Ambition"

Odontoglossum Species

BICTONIENSE. An old favourite, collected from high altitudes of the Andes mountain range. The leaves are stiff, pointed and succulent, suggesting that this species is well equipped to withstand extremes of temperature. The main attraction in this species is the beautifully heart-shaped lip, coloured rose, contrasting with the smaller whitish sepals and petals. The flowers, about 1½ inches across, are evenly and alternately spaced out on a stout, erect stem, growing to a length of 3 feet under good cultivation. An ideal odontoglossum for an amateur's mixed collection.

CITROSMUM. The drooping, often branched spikes carry numerous rounded and scented flowers, sporting a prominent purple lip with yellow crest, against a white or buff background provided by the sepals and petals. It comes from Mexico and is therefore used to warmer and drier conditions. Altogether a desirable species for the amateur.

CRISPUM. A very variable species from Colombia, extensively used by the hybridizers on account of its large, well-balanced flowers. The numerous coloured varieties have been largely superseded by improved hybrids, but the white forms with golden crested, often fringed, lips, are still the most popular of all the odontoglossum species. A new race of this species has been evolved by Messrs. Charlesworth, called Crispum Premier, by intercrossing the best forms of white crispums. The lip and petals may be beautifully rounded by unbroken borders, or heavily fringed and ruffled. They may be chaste white or suffused with a purple sheen, or carry small rounded red-brown spots, sometimes singly, sometimes in clusters, but all are endowed with that beautiful golden-yellow crest on the lip and a glistening, waxy appearance. A group of Crispum Premier type, with arching spikes of 2 and 3 feet in length, never fails to attract attention and is a highly desirable acquisition. The plants in cultivation are apt to overtax themselves and shrivelling of the bulbs is a natural corollary of their herculean effort of producing long spikes with numerous large flowers often in excess of 3 inches in diameter. The variety Xanthotes has yellow spots on a white background on rather smaller flowers, but its constitution leaves much to be desired from the amateur's point of view.

EDWARDII. Here we have another good-natured, desirable subject for the mixed collection, on account of its strongly scented, numerous flowers carried on branched spikes up to 4 feet in length. Found in Ecuador on the lower slopes of the Andes, the flowers are barred chestnut brown on buff or yellowish background, with a mauve-purple lip, crested yellow. Unfortunately, rare in this country.

HARRYANUM. The characteristics of this species can be traced in many a hybrid owing to the peculiar elongated shape of the flower, apart from their striking colouring. The sepals and petals are waved, of a glossy brown, relieved by streaks of greenish yellow, whilst the elongated lip is coloured white, yellow and brown with purple veining, capped by a deep yellow crest—a truly striking combination. Originates from Colombia.

LUTEO-PURPUREUM. Another attractive, if variable, species from Colombia, producing large, somewhat star-shaped flowers on arching spikes. The wavy sepals are marked with a glossy red-brown, margined and tipped bright yellow. The petals are fringed and spotted red-brown on a yellow background. The large fringed lip is yellow with purple spots.

NOBILE, alias PESCATOREI. Introduced from Colombia, better known under the name of Pescatorei. Of floriferous habit, producing numerous 3-inch white flowers on arching, branched spikes. The sepals and petals are of a clear white in some and suffused with light purple in others. The lip is white with purple and sometimes crimson spots.

PULCHELLUM. From Guatemala, the fragrance of its small, rounded, white flowers, about half a dozen in number, makes this another desirable species for those who appreciate scented orchids.

ROSSII. A diminutive but charming species from Mexico, which few can resist on account of its charming shapely flowers, towering above the tiny bulbs and short narrow leaves. It is easy to grow and to flower in a mixed collection and the flowers are exceptionally long lasting. The pointed sepals are white or cream coloured, blotched or barred with chestnut brown, and the petals are slightly recurved, white with a few basal spots of brown. A comparatively large, wavy lip of pure white, with a yellow crest, completes a very charming picture.

TRIUMPHANS. A Colombian species, with arge yellow and red-brown flowers with creamy-white, purple-blotched lip. This species has been freely used by the hybridizers in the production of yellow hybrids and is a very showy and attractive addition to any collection.

URO-SKINNERII. This once very popular species is not met with so frequently today, although it deserves a place in every collection. Its well-shaped flowers are 2 inches across, produced in liberal numbers on long, erect spikes up to 3 feet in length. The sepals and petals are of a greenish colour, mottled chestnut-brown, and the equally striking flat and heart-shaped lip is rose-coloured with white mottling.

Odontoglossum Grande

How this show-piece from Guatemala came to be assigned to the odontoglossum tribe only the botanists can explain. The shape and formation of the bulbs, leaves and flowers are totally different from those of the tribe, as are the cultural requirements of the Grande. It is, in fact, more at home among the lælias in a cattleya house than in one devoted to odontoglossums. Indifferent to extremes of temperature and to the glare of the sun, short of scorching, O. *Grande* has a decided period of rest after flowering, when watering should be gradually reduced and withheld altogether upon completion of the newly made up bulb. Give no water at all in December and January and very little afterwards until the new growth is well on the way. Repot in the spring, when new growth has started again, and use more fibre than moss—about two parts of fibre to one part of moss.

It is an ideal beginner's orchid and quickly grows into a specimen plant, with four to five large blooms per spike, some 5 inches across or more, which can best be described as "glamorous." The sepals are of a rich yellow colour, irregularly barred with a glossy chestnut-brown, whilst the colours of the petals are almost equally divided into a brown base and yellow outer half. The well-rounded, creamy lip is prettily marked with a red-brown pattern and golden-yellow crest.

ODONTIODA

Although this was before my time as an amateur orchid grower, I can well imagine the excitement that the appearance of the first bigeneric cross between an odontoglossum and a cochlioda must have caused. The "shot" of new colours imparted to the odontoglossum tribe by this momentous advent triggered off a new race known as odontiodas. The shape of the odontoglossum flower was hardly affected by this "inoculation," but the orange-scarlet of the cochlioda endowed it with darker, more vivid and varied colours. Little wonder then that hundreds of such crosses have been made since, which have found their way into and enriched odontoglossum collections as inseparable cousins.

The smaller flowers of the earlier odontiodas made up in numbers for what they lacked in size, having inherited the branched habit of the cochlioda. By the inevitable process of interbreeding, the size of the odontioda flowers in the later hybrids has been brought well up to the standard of the odontoglossum and the two genera are often hardly distinguishable, except for the presence of deep-red colouring in the odontioda. Generally speaking, the odontioda is more robust than its cousin and less exacting in its cultural requirements. The discerning eye can often distinguish prospering odontiodas with large fat bulbs from lean odontoglossum growths in the same collection.

ODONTONIA

Another bigeneric cross, this time between odontoglossum and miltonia. A desirable but very difficult cross indeed, in which the enterprising amateur may like to try his hand. A swelling calyx may give an indication that the cross has "taken"—*i.e.*, that the pollination has been successful. Excitement runs high and inspection of the swelling seed pod is made at frequent intervals. The fact that you have made a "successful" odontonia cross is freely publicized, until, possibly four or five weeks later, your hopes are shattered by the sight of that insidious yellowing of the stem below the calyx. What an elusive, hopeless cross! That was the ninety-ninth try and still nothing to show. Still, with the gambler's instinct, more or less dormant in all of us, mingled with a dogged determination to get your own back, you have another go, and another, until one day, who knows? Only once so far did I succeed in ripening an odontonia seed pod, but I am still waiting for the seedlings to come up!

What makes the odontonia such a desirable cross? The only good thing that comes out of this bigeneric cross is an enlarged lip with the sepals and petals akin to its odontoglossum parent—

if you're lucky! Sometimes the generous proportions of the lip are quite unsupported by the other segments and burning is the only sensible sequel. When you hit the jackpot, however, and produce a well-proportioned odontonia, you are not likely to be forgotten in a hurry by your orchid-growing friends!

The odontonia takes after its miltonia parent as far as its cultural preferences are concerned and is thus more at home in the miltonia or cypripedium house than in the odontoglossum section. It likes more warmth than the odontoglossum, especially when artificial heat is employed, and is therefore easier to grow in warmer climates than the latter. Its scarcity is due not only to the inherent difficulty of this combination but also to its reluctance in producing fertile seeds, which are therefore few in number. So very few plants of this bigeneric cross being available today, no good purpose can be served by listing the few successful crosses made in the past.

ODONTOCIDIUM

This bigeneric cross between odontoglossum and oncidium suggests possibilities for the enterprising hybridizer, on account of its numerous colourful flowers, usually carried on long, branching spikes. Its home is the odontoglossum house, but it should do well in a mixed collection.

VUYLSTEKEARA

A trigeneric cross comprising the three genera odontoglossum, cochlioda and miltonia—*i.e.*, between odontioda and miltonia or miltonioda and odontoglossum. Fertile seeds of this cross are as hard to come by as they are with the odontonia, which also share their cultural requirements. The flowers are usually on the small side, but numerous and vividly coloured, red preponderating.

WILSONARA

A trigeneric combination of odontoglossum, cochlioda and oncidium, wilsonara is obtained by crossing odontioda with oncidium or odontocidium with cochlioda or oncidioda with odontoglossum. The flowers are small, but numerous and brightly coloured, carried on stout, erect stems, usually branched. Hybrids of this group make good growers, not too exacting, and should give a good account of themselves either in the odontoglossum house or in a mixed collection.

BURRAGEARA

A quadrigeneric mixture of odontoglossum, cochlioda, oncidium and miltonia, resulting from a cross that comprises any combination of the four named genera and hybrids. Owing to the influence of miltonia in its make-up, burrageara hybrids appreciate a little more warmth than provided in the odontoglossum house in the winter and should, therefore, be grown with the miltonias or cypripediums. Very few hybrids of this group have been raised, leaving plenty of scope to the amateur who is attracted by novel and rare crosses.

11

CYMBIDIUM

UNQUESTIONABLY the most popular orchid family in this country today is the cymbidium tribe. The attractive, evergreen, palm-like foliage, fanned out in arching fashion, is in itself an invitation to grow cymbidiums in preference to many foliage plants. Added to the elegance of the plant's appearance is the promise of 3 to 5 feet long spikes with numerous large flowers of every colour with the exception of blue and crimson. But the attraction of the cymbidium does not finish there. Whilst most of the other tribes of orchids require a fairly high temperature, cymbidiums will flourish under cool conditions—a truly attractive proposition in view of the high cost of fuels today. It may well be that this is the greatest contributory factor to the popularity cymbidiums enjoy today in this country.

Like all good things, however, they have their limitations, and the would-be grower is therefore well advised to carefully weigh up all the factors before selling out in favour of cymbidiums. A small house with a low roof, for instance, is not suitable for housing them. Once the seedlings or small plants have grown up, they require a considerable amount of space. When the foliage has reached the roof it is liable to get scorched, even if the house is normally shaded. The plants will not like overheated or stuffy conditions, such as one frequently encounters in small houses. Except under ideal growing conditions, even adult and well-developed plants may "hang fire" for two or three years without obliging with a single flower spike. Many seedlings reach the age of seven or eight years before they begin to think of flowering.

Far be it from me to discourage anybody, but if my own experience is anything to go by, growing cymbidiums should not be attempted in small houses or severely restricted spaces. Like most amateurs, I "fell" for the cymbidium right from the start. All went well for some years, as my plants flowered well and regularly. Having used up all available space for extensions (and my collection of various genera, like all collections, had a habit of growing), overcrowding was inevitable. The time came, a few years ago, when I had to decide what had to go to relieve congestion and to make management of the plants a less laborious pastime. The cymbidiums were the chief culprits—and it was the cymbidiums that went—I have often missed them, but the fact remains that each cymbidium made room for half a dozen odontoglossums, miltonias or cypripediums.

Planning from the start would have prevented the loss incurred, but such is the power of attraction of the cymbidium that planning went by the board. This may, if to a lesser extent, apply to other genera, of course, such as the oncidiums, which may produce flower spikes 6 or 7 feet in length. For the benefit of those who have the space and patience to grow these beautiful plants from the seedling stage, I will describe in the following pages the method of culture, which has produced flower spikes with unfailing regularity.

Contrary to a widespread impression, cymbidiums are epiphytic and not terrestrial orchids, although some may occasionally be found growing on the ground. Their native habitat extends from the foothills of the Himalayas down to Burma, growing in high elevations. With the exception of *C. giganteum*, *C. Lowianum* var. *grandiflorum* and the sweetly scented *C. Tracyanum*, the species are seldom met with under cultivation, having been superseded by the better forms and colouring of the much improved modern hybrids.

The main flowering season of the cymbidium hybrids lies between January and April, but the hybridists are endeavouring to advance, or extend, the flowering season of the genera by back-crossing with early- or late-flowering species and hybrids. Bearing in mind, however, that the cymbidium flowers will last in good condition up to three months, an impressive display of blooms and colour can be had for several months.

TEMPERATURE AND SHADING

As in the case of the odontoglossum, the modern cymbidium hybrids bred in this country from established and thoroughly acclimatized parents have little in common with their ancestors as far as their cultural requirements are concerned. That is just as well, as it is extremely difficult to reproduce in this country's variable climate the atmospheric conditions prevailing at the high altitudes of their natural habitat. Cymbidiums are cool-growing

PLATE XLIV. Dendrobium "Fimbriatum," var. Oculatum

PLATE XLV. Cypripedium "A. Lomax," Whitton var.

PLATE XL
Cypripedi
"Spring Sc

PLATE XL
Cypripedi
"Golden W

PLATE XLV
Cypripedi
"Wyndhar
var. Heathf

orchids and it is easy to provide near-ideal conditions when fire heat is applied during cold weather. A night temperature of around 50° F., with a rise of 8° to 10° F. in daytime, is all they require. If a day temperature in that region cannot be maintained, it is better to drop the night temperature by a corresponding number of degrees. The variation in day and night temperatures is of the utmost importance if they are expected to flower. Keeping the plants comfortable in hot weather, when the temperature will on occasions soar into the eighties, is a different matter. Effective shading will considerably ease this task and provides the only real remedy. Constant damping down and spraying will only result in a moisture-saturated atmosphere and the close conditions so inimical to the health of these plants. Lath blinds are ideal for the cymbidium house in the spring and autumn, but not sufficient for keeping the plants cool in hot summer weather. A lining of Windolite or Polythene on the roof will add to the effectiveness of the lath blinds, but in their absence the roof must be painted over with "permanent" shading distemper, preferably "Videnor." The heavy shading should be gradually reduced, however, as soon as it is safe to do so, depending on the prevailing weather conditions, otherwise the new growths will not ripen off sufficiently to induce the plants to flower. Lath blinds enable the grower to take into account existing weather conditions and to take advantage of all suitable occasions for admitting as much light into the cymbidium house as is consistent with safety. Pulling the blinds over the roof before the sun has settled on it, if necessary last thing at night, will keep the house cool for many hours. If chances have to be taken by the owner who is away from home all day, let the shading be in excess, rather than the reverse.

VENTILATION AND ATMOSPHERIC MOISTURE

The cymbidium produces more leaves per growth, and certainly more leaf surface, than any other orchid of similar dimensions. With its gorgeous breathing apparatus, it is well equipped to take advantage of beneficial atmospheric conditions and to cope with an abundance of fresh air. Observation will confirm that this genus flowers more freely in a large, high-roofed house than in a small, closely confined structure, where the plants are in close proximity to the pipes. Whilst the large, roomy house largely takes care of its own ventilation, this must be conscientiously attended to in the smaller house. For once, a little draught here and there, except in very cold weather, does no harm and the gently swaying leaves seem to nod their approval.

The ventilators should be kept open, if only an inch or two, day and night, whenever the requisite temperature has been reached. In congenial weather, especially when dew can be expected at night, the ventilators can be left wide open and very little damping down is required. On close nights or when fire heat has to be employed the required atmospheric moisture has to be created artificially by damping down the floor and closing the ventilators after sunset in the evening. Open the ventilators again in the morning, by degrees, increasing ventilation as the thermometer rises. The aim is to provide the plants with drier and warmer conditions in daytime, to assist transpiration of the leaves.

POTTING MATERIALS AND REPOTTING

Cymbidiums have long, fleshy roots and do best in a root-bound condition. The roots make for the airiest places, that is, near the pot edge, trailing round and round the ball of compost, eventually weaving a solid mat of roots and completely hiding the compost. This is not a sign that the plant needs repotting, but one of good culture. The roots are thus in the best position to receive simultaneous supplies of air and moisture, whilst escaping any waterlogged condition of a decayed or decaying compost. The plants should therefore only be repotted when (*a*) the compost is impoverished, (*b*) the roots have decayed through overwatering, (*c*) the leading bulb has reached the pot edge, (*d*) divisions are needed for propagation purposes.

In the first two cases, (*a*) and (*b*), remove as much of the old compost as possible without damaging any live roots and cut back all decayed roots, except those needed for anchorage. Replace with fresh compost and repot in the same size pot, or slightly smaller. The compost in this case should be made up of two parts of osmunda fibre to one part of sphagnum moss, with a few flaked oak leaves or pieces of tan bark added. Where "dropping on" only is needed (*c*), soak the plant before knocking out of the pot, to release the roots clinging to the latter, and repot in a slightly larger pot, mixing small pieces of fibrous loam with the compost suggested for (*a*) and (*b*). The size of the pot should allow for two years' development—*i.e.*, for two new bulbs. When plants have to be divided (*d*), or back-bulbs removed, cut through the rhizome in front of the bulbs to be removed and tear apart. Some of the roots will be damaged in the process, but not to the same extent as when the knife is pushed right through the compost. Pot up the major portion as suggested for (*c*) and the back-bulbs in an equal mixture of fibre and moss.

In all cases ample drainage must be provided to allow surplus water to run away freely, at the same time ensuring good aeration, the importance of which cannot be overstressed. Stand the pot-sherds on end vertically, to enable the roots to get between them. When potting up well-rooted plants, sprinkle a pinch of hoof and horn meal over the new compost in the bottom half of the pot. It constitutes an innocuous, slow feed and, if mixed with crushed potsherds or brick rubble, helps drainage and aeration. As a safeguard against the effects of overwatering, powdered or crushed charcoal can be added to the compost. Both hoof and horn meal and charcoal should be added as potting proceeds, as they do not readily mix with the compost.

WATERING

Whichever method of watering one prefers, care must be taken that the centre of the compost dries out between each application, otherwise it will soon be reduced to an unhealthy state. If the surface of the compost is slightly domed and sloping down towards the edge of the pot, most of the water applied overhead will drain away towards the edge of the pot, as it should. Immersion of the plant, up to one-quarter of its depth from the pot rim, may be a safer method of watering for the inexperienced and the surface layer of compost will remain in a healthy state. Frequent overhead watering encourages lichenous growths on the surface of the plants, turning the compost sour for lack of aeration.

Each plant should be inspected once a week during the summer months to ascertain its water requirements by lifting, and once every fortnight during the winter months. Plants developing flower spikes must receive particular attention, as they must not be allowed to dry right out.

PLANTS IN SPIKE

During the months of August and September, rather drier conditions should be aimed at to encourage the development of flower spikes. Water at longer intervals during these months until the plants have shown their intentions either to flower or to break into growth again. It is not always possible in the early stages to distinguish between flower spikes and new growths. The former are usually stubby, with rounded tops, whilst the latter are pointed. Keep the flowering plants reasonably moist and the non-flowering ones reasonably dry, but do not allow the bulbs to shrivel.

When the spikes have grown a few inches, a stout stake should be provided as a guard against accidental damage in the first place, and for supporting the spike later on. Do not tie the spike tightly to the stake, however, and allow the spike to develop in its natural way. Some of the cymbidiums will produce straight, erect spikes growing vertically, whilst others will grow outwards at all angles in graceful arching fashion. As the spike extends and gains in weight, another tie, preferably below the lowest bud, should be provided. When the flowers are fully developed, give extra shading to preserve them as long as possible and reduce the frequency of watering, the plant having arrived at a semi-quiescent stage. The plants should be relieved of their spikes after one month and, placed in narrow-necked vases filled with rainwater and arranged among the other plants in flower, they will contribute to the floral display for a few more weeks.

12

CYPRIPEDIUM

THIS is a very large genus, botanically divided into paphiopedilum, widely distributed over the East Asiatic sphere; selenipedium, originating from South America; and cypripedium, referring to the hardy type of the lady slipper orchid. Whilst this book is not concerned with the latter, however varied and fascinating they may be, the name cypripedium, or more commonly referred to as "cyps," has nevertheless "stuck" in this country and covers all types in this genus under cultivation. It is quite different from all other genera of the orchid family and very popular with collectors all over the world, as well as with florists. The cypripedium is often classed as a connoisseur's orchid, probably because of the unique and interesting structure of the flowers which are more interesting than "showy" when compared with the floral display of other genera. Their undisputed individuality and aristocratic mien have a singularly magnetic appeal that does not depend on numbers or effect of mass display. Once they get established in your orchid house, they are there for "keeps," whatever happens to the members of other genera present.

The small amount of space a cypripedium plant claims, makes it possible to grow a surprising number of plants even in a small house. Their cultivation does not call for consummate skill on the part of the amateur and the flowers will last up to three months, according to variety and treatment. A cypripedium hybrid of mine with two blooms open on Christmas Day, exhibited in January, again in February and again at an orchid show in mid-March, will illustrate this. Not even the vagaries of the journeys in cold, wintry weather had any effect on the blooms! The cool-growing varieties make ideal beginners' plants, especially as they flower quite early in life and continue to flower with unfailing regularity, given a modicum of congenial treatment.

For the purposes of cultural treatment, we have to divide the cypripedium into two classes—viz., the green-leaved or cool-growing kind, and the mottled or tessellated-leaved variety, which requires warmer and moister atmospheric conditions coupled with more intense shading. For growing in small houses, or mixed collections, the amateur is advised to keep to the green-leaved variety, which may come into bloom at any time between September and May the following year. The plants seldom growing above 1 ft. in height, or the leaves more than 1 ft. in length, smallish structures are quite suitable for the cultivation of cypripediums.

Whilst modern hybrids will form the bulk of the collection, the genus cypripedium contains many species of modest dimensions which are veritable gems, usually quite inexpensive, and these have a habit of finding their way into collections, in spite of the advances made in hybridizing. The colours of the cypripedium tribe are not so numerous or pronounced as they are found in other genera and most will be found in shades of green, brown, white, reddish-purple and yellow, but their unique veining in shades of green and purple, or spotting with purple or chocolate brown, often to the extent of forming small protuberances, is very effective. Again, the smooth, polished appearance of the elaborately shaped pouch or labellum forms a vivid contrast to its spotted, veined or streaked background. The kingpin and chief target of the hybridizers, however, is the dorsal sepal, which rises like a flag above the vitals of the flower and determines the price of the modern hybrid more than any other factor.

TEMPERATURE AND SHADING

Generally speaking, these terrestrial orchids appreciate warmth and shade more than is commonly realized, especially where modern hybrids are concerned. A good display of blooms by the green-leaved cypripediums can be had with a minimum winter temperature of 55° F., with an occasional drop to 50° F., but they will grow at a faster pace if the temperature can be maintained around 60° F. The day temperature, however, should exceed the night temperature by at least 5° F., which would bring the day temperature up to a minimum of 65° F. Few amateurs can maintain such a high temperature by fire-heat only and it is better in such cases to allow the night temperature to fall to a lower level, in order to bring about the essential alternation between day and night temperatures. With sun heat, cypripediums are quite happy with an increase of 20° F. in daytime.

The tessellated-leaved varieties, which comprises the Maudiæ group, will not grow satisfactorily below a minimum temperature of 60° F. A glass case or propagating frame inside the cypripedium house, heated by a mere 60-watt lamp, can help the amateur over this difficulty and enable him to bring these attractive plants safely through the winter. The foliage is attractive enough to install such a glass case in the living room, but in this case thermostatic control should be fitted. A glass partition near the warmer end of the cypripedium house has brought about the same desired results within my own ken. These beautiful mottled-leaved plants are worth growing for their foliage alone and are well worth a little trouble to make them comfortable.

Shading must be fairly heavy during the hot summer months and I can think of no better form than that provided by Pinolium blinds. Lath blinds alone do not provide sufficient shading in bright weather and must be supplemented by a thin coat of distemper on the roof, or Windolite or Polythene sheeting. With the help of the latter protection, the lath blinds can be dispensed with from October onwards to the following March or April, according to weather conditions.

VENTILATION AND ATMOSPHERIC MOISTURE

Ventilation in the cypripedium house is in the main limited to the function of regulating the moisture content in the air. For this reason, and for the purpose of reducing the moisture content in daytime, the ventilators should be opened in the morning as soon as the requisite day temperature has been reached. In the evening, preferably before the sun has left the house, the ventilators should be closed again and the blinds withdrawn, in order to induce the moisture in the house to rise into the air and also to conserve as much natural warmth as possible. If a number of plants have been watered during the day, and provided there are no leaks in the glass structure, this will be sufficient to provide the requisite atmospheric moisture for the night, otherwise the floor should be damped down after closing the ventilators last thing at night. The drier atmosphere in daytime has the visible effect of firming-up the leaves, which would otherwise remain weak and floppy, but they must be provided with atmospheric moisture at night for their sustenance and growth.

POTTING MATERIALS AND REPOTTING

A reliable potting medium is a mixture of two parts of osmunda fibre, chopped up fairly small, one part of sphagnum moss, one part of fibrous loam, one handful of flaked oak leaves or two handfuls of acid-free tan bark per gallon of compost. A pinch or two of granulated or powdered charcoal will keep the compost in a "sweet" condition for a long period and is a safeguard for the consequences of excessive or too frequent watering. A small handful of brick or limestone rubble added while potting is in progress will keep the compost open and assist aeration. Ample drainage must be provided by standing on edge pieces of pot-sherds over the drainage crock.

The fleshy, hairy cypripedium roots depend for their existence as much on air as they do on moisture. They thrive best among the crocks, where they have free access to both. If the plants are watered from the top, the roots will be found as much on or near the surface, often trailing round the pot rim, as inside the edge of the pot. This preference for the "wide open spaces" is an indication of their eminent need for good aeration. When a plant is repotted, which is best done soon after flowering, it will be found that the roots in the centre of the compost have decayed and not those that have free access to the air. Do not therefore overpot or ram the compost down into the pot, but only firm enough to hold the plant steady. The base of the growths should be slightly buried in the surface layer of the compost to encourage new roots, and if the plant is surfaced in the manner described earlier on, the danger of decay is very remote.

When a plant has to be divided, do not push the knife down the compost, but only as far as is necessary to separate the growths, taking care not to damage these or their roots. Remove the crocks and pull the plant apart by gripping each division firmly in your hands. It will be found that the roots will disentangle themselves and the decayed portions of compost can then be safely teased out without damaging any live roots. Cut off all decayed roots and build the new compost up among the new roots, without forcing them into unaccustomed positions. It is not necessary to place fresh compost underneath the roots at the bottom of the pot, otherwise it will be found wanting in depth. It is bad practice to cut or shorten live roots on cypripediums in order to force them into the compost or to facilitate the operation.

Cypripediums do not make many roots and the plants depend on every one of them for their recovery and future progress. Their roots do not branch as readily as they do with other genera, when cut, and they are likely to rot off, especially when surrounded with compost.

Shade heavily newly potted plants or divisions, and if a place under the staging can be found for them not too close to the pipes when heated, they will also escape any accidental watering. If by any chance plants or divisions have lost their roots, anchorage has to be improvised by stakes and ties, forcing the base of the growths into the compost without burying the new growths.

WATERING

A weekly inspection will not find these plants gasping for water at any time of the year, and only after the second or third inspection will they feel light enough to warrant partial immersion during the cold or dull seasons. Whether watered by immersion or with a can from the top, make sure the plant feels light when lifted before soaking it. If a plant feels heavy, or a doubt exists as to its state of dryness, the golden rule is to put it back on the stage unwatered. Little dribbles of water are no help to the plant and may only lead to a similar state of uncertainty at the following inspection. The absence of pseudo-bulbs does not imply, as so often erroneously assumed, that the compost of a cypripedium plant has to be kept constantly wet. The fleshy roots and succulent leaves in numbers, are in themselves storehouses of moisture. A prolonged wet state of the compost is far worse in its effect than the opposite, as experiments on these lines have proved. A semi-dry state, in which the roots have to grow in search of moisture, is the ideal to be aimed at.

Newly potted plants or divisions do not need any watering for two or three weeks and then only if live roots are present in the compost. Rootless plants should only be "dewed" over with a mist-like spray, until new roots appear from the base of the growths. This may take two or three months, hence the desirability for segregating such plants.

PLANTS IN BUD AND FLOWER

The flower buds are visible long before they emerge from the centre of the growths. Until they have done so, the danger of rotting off is ever present, and many a disappointment has been caused by the loss of buds which, in most cases, could have been avoided. Overmoist conditions, drips from the roof, spraying overhead and cold draughts are the chief culprits. I do not know what good overhead spraying is supposed to do to established cypripedium plants, but it is a widespread practice. Not only the buds but the centre of the growth can decay if water is allowed to lodge in it at low temperatures.

When the bud has successfully emerged from the growth, see that the leaves of neighbouring growths do not cross its path and that its stem is free to grow vertically upwards, unobstructed. It may be necessary to deflect some leaves with thin stakes—a worthwhile attention, considering the ugly sight of a bent or twisted stem. A weakly stem, usually the result of high temperature-cum-moisture culture, may itself have to be staked and secured with a tie, but do not provide the final tie around the calyx until the flower has fully expanded. From the time the bud starts to open to the setting of the flower, the plants should be left in the same position in relation to the sun, otherwise some of the segments may be drawn out of position and the flowers deformed. Study the position of the bud from an early stage and turn the plant round if it is necessary or desirable to draw the bud into a different direction, from where the flower can be admired free from obstruction. The flowers will last longer if kept cool and well-shaded and the plants can be safely taken indoors at this stage.

Cypripedium Species

BARBATUM. A warm-growing species from Malaya. The rounded dorsal sepal is pleated in the centre, white, striped purple, green at the base. The upper margins of the petals are hairy and dotted with dark-coloured warts, brownish-green towards the base and purple near the tips. The glossy lip is of purple-brown colouring and the leaves are mottled.

BELLATULUM. A strikingly bold flower carried on short stems, with exceptionally wide petals and, like the cupped, wide dorsal sepal, white or pale yellow, spotted dark purple. The small, burnished lip is white or creamy white and the long wide leaves are dark green with lighter green mottling on the surface and purple shading underneath. From South China, notably Malacca, it requires a fairly high temperature to grow well.

CALLOSUM. The flowers are carried on long stems and dominated by a large and strikingly veined dorsal sepal, pleated in the centre, the veins changing from purple to green at the base. The petals are of a pale green with purple tips and carry a number of blackish warts on the upper margin. The lip is of brownish-purple colouring with a green base and has dark purple spots on the side lobes. A native of Siam, it belongs to the warm-growing, mottled-leaved variety.

CURTISII. The vividly tessellated, light-coloured leaves give this species from Sumatra an attractive appearance, even when not in flower. It is therefore a desirable acquisition for the warm section of the cypripedium house, particularly its variety *Sanderæ,* with its light green or greenish-yellow flowers with a wide, white margin on the dorsal sepal, greenish warts on the upper fringe of the petals and smooth shapely lip.

FAIRIEANUM. A most fascinating, green-leaved species from Assam that never fails to attract attention on account of its unusual, elongated, graceful shape and vividly reticulated colour pattern. Not difficult to grow, it usually succeeds in a mixed collection. It flowers at all times of the year, if allowed to grow into a large plant, but resents division. The dorsal sepal is oblong, almost square in shape, overlapping and undulated at the top, with a white ground colour and beautifully and prominently patterned with a purple reticulation, almost bordering on crimson in some varieties. The petals are of a pale yellow colour, veined purple, hairy and undulated at the margins, with the tips gracefully curved upwards. The narrow lip is of greenish colour, also reticulated purple.

HIRSUTISSIMUM. Another distinct and eye-catching, green-leaved species from Assam, the flowers and stems of which are covered with blackish hairs. The dorsal sepal is veined dark purple on a green background. The twisted petals are undulating, spotted dark purple on a green base, the lip green with purple suffusion.

INSIGNE. The beginner's ideal guinea-pig that grows under cool conditions and is quite amenable to room-culture. A fast grower, which soon grows into a large specimen plant in a compost with higher-than-usual loam content. The lower half of the dorsal sepal is green and the upper half white, both heavily spotted purple-brown. The petals are light green with brown or purple veins, whilst the prominent lip is pale green or yellowish-green shaded with brown. There are many variations in form and colouring, as there are in its variety *Sanderæ*, the colour of which ranges from pale to deep yellow, except for the apical portion of the dorsal sepal.

LAWRENCEANUM. A native of Borneo, with bright tessellated leaves, requiring a fairly high temperature. The large flowers have well-rounded, flat dorsal sepals, white, symmetrically veined purple. The green, purple-tipped petals are fringed with hairy black warts and the lip is large and of a purple-brown shading.

NIVEUM. A small gem from the Loncavi Islands, one of the group of white species, with small purple spots, of good shape and substance, the small lip presenting a polished appearance. The leaves are mottled and, like the back of the dorsal sepal, shaded with bright purple.

ROTHSCHILDIANUM. An imposing plant in and out of flower, with its long, substantial green foliage and multi-flowered tall stems, bearing two or three large remarkably shaped and coloured flowers. The dorsal sepal is yellow, striped with black-purple and the long, narrow petals are pale green with purple spots and fine, dark green veining. The large, prominent lip is coloured red-brown, veined purple, with a yellow rim, jutting out in a challenging fashion. Found in the Dutch East Indies and well worth a place in the cypripedium collection.

SANDERIANUM. A Malayan species, noted for the remarkable length of its narrow, twisted petals, from 1½ to 2 feet in length, of a yellowish colour, barred and spotted purple. The pointed dorsal sepal is greenish-yellow with brown stripes. The large, projecting lip is yellow at the base and brownish-purple above.

SPICERIANUM. The outstanding feature of this attractive species is its broad white dorsal sepal, with reddish-purple dividing line down the centre and a green base. The petals have wavy fringes and the pale green colouring is divided into upper and lower halves by a central purple line. The long, graceful lip is purple-brown with green suffusion. Many a modern hybrid owes these attractive features to this species from Assam.

STONEI. A very interesting introduction from the Dutch East

Indies, with picturesque large flowers, carried up to five in number on tall, erect stems. The dorsal sepal is white with deep purple streaks and the long, twisted petals are tawny coloured, except for its crimson tips, with a few reddish-brown spots. The projecting lip is rose coloured with crimson reticulations.

VILLOSUM. An easily grown species from Moulmein which soon grows into large specimen plants; green-leaved, with purple backing. The flowers are large, hairy and covered with a glossy sheen and the colours are enhanced in the well-known variety *Boxallii*, which has been extensively used as a parent. The narrow-waisted dorsal sepal is green and brownish-purple, tipped white. The wavy petals are brown-yellow, with a central line of purple. The well-shaped lip is yellowish-brown with clear yellow rim.

13

CATTLEYA

Undeniably the "showiest" and largest single blooms belong to hybrids of the cattleya group. The numerous species, which in years gone by have caused so much excitement when first introduced, have been well and truly eclipsed by a superior race of cattleyas, thanks to the efforts of the hybridists. Orchidists with nostalgic leanings towards species will still find a number of these in circulation, but such vast numbers of improved hybrids have been produced in this country alone that the former have even lost the advantage of price. Whether we like it or not, we have to face the fact that species of the cattleya tribe are fast disappearing from our collections, making room for our many hundreds of hybrids, improved in size, shape and colouring. Whilst the hybridist still has to fall back occasionally on the species to reinvigorate the constitution of highly involved and interbred hybrids, the amateur today has an inexhaustible choice of hybrids of all colours, sizes and shapes.

But the advantage of our modern hybrids is not confined to their appearance alone. They are easier to manage and the traditional resting periods of the species have been bred out of them, so much so that many of the hybrids can be got to flower twice in twelve months. The specialized knowledge needed for the treatment of species is not essential in a collection of hybrids and any amateur can achieve success with these easily grown plants, given a modicum of understanding. Provided a minimum temperature of 55° F. can be maintained during the winter months, they should give a good account of themselves even in a mixed collection.

Cattleyas have long, stout pseudo-bulbs growing out of equally robust rhizomes, large succulent leaves and thick, fleshy roots, and are thus well equipped to withstand periods of drought—or cultural errors at the hands of the inexperienced. The vast majority of the plants produce one single leaf at the apex of the pseudo-bulb and these owe their ancestry to the labiata group of cattleyas. The twin-leaved group produce smaller flowers, but usually make up in number what they lack in size. The pseudobulbs of the latter group are longer and thinner. Both these groups have been interbred, mingling their characteristics to such an extent that the same hybrid often produces single and twin leaves in succession, or simultaneously on different growths. Each bulb has two "eyes" at the base above the rhizome, one or both of which will grow into a new bulb. The more warmth and light that can be given to the plant, the better the chances are for developing both "eyes" into new growths. Any mishap that may befall the leading growth and stop it from growing will invariably excite the second "eye" into growth, thus providing a second chance. Sometimes the dormant "eyes" on the back-bulbs will start into growth, but these generally need two or three years to develop into flowering bulbs. Manuring often brings about this development of tributary growths, at the expense of the leading growth.

MULTI-GENERIC HYBRIDS

The vast diversity in size, shape and colour in cattleya blooms has received a new and far-reaching impetus, when it was discovered many years ago that they freely interbreed with members of related genera. The large, gorgeously frilled lip of the brassavola has thus transferred these beautiful characteristics to the cattleya, by intercrossing these two genera, giving birth to a new bigeneric race called brassocattleya. A similar process has endowed many cattleya hybrids with scent, floriferousness, different shapes and colouring, notably in the lip, by intercrossing with members of the lælia family, and these bigeneric hybrids are known as læliocattleya. Following in the wake of these bigeneric crosses was the fusion of all three genera mentioned, resulting in the appearance of the gorgeous trigeneric race called brassolæliocattleya. Not satisfied with the magnificent results already achieved, the vivid scarlet-red of the *Sophronitis Grandiflora* was taken advantage of by interbreeding with members of the cattleya family and their hybrids, and so was born the brilliantly coloured bigeneric sophrocattleya, the trigeneric sophrolæliocattleya and the quadrigeneric potinara, which includes all four members of the abovenamed genera.

These interbreeding activities have been going on for a long time and have not all come out on the credit side; far from it. The bad points of a parent are just as liable to be conveyed to its offspring as are the good ones. Thus scent has been lost, desirable characteristics have been obliterated by the preponderance of others, shape and size have deteriorated in some hybrids, and some of the plants themselves have been reduced to a fraction of the size of some of their progenitors. It does not, therefore, follow as a matter of course that a BLC is better than a LC, or that a potinara is better than a BLC, and so forth, although this may be the case in some of the hybrids. An undeniable outcome of this high-pressure hybridizing, however, is the immense variety available today to the lovers of cattleyas, and for this we have to be grateful to the hybridizers, quite apart from any advances made in the quality of the blooms.

The cultural requirements of these generic hybrids do not vary sufficiently to warrant different or separate treatment and are, therefore, dealt with collectively. The amateur with barely sufficient heat at his command to maintain a reasonable minimum, however, is advised to leave the hybrids with brassavola influence —viz., BC, BLC, and Potinara—out of his collection. The brassavola is a notorious heat lover and this issue cannot be side-tracked. The same applies to the yellow hybrids, probably due to the *C. Dowiana Aurea* influence, as the blooms seldom develop satisfactorily in persistently low temperatures. The *Sophronitis Grandiflora* has not imparted any exaggerated flowering propensity to its SC, SLC and potinara descendants and a position near the roof glass will give them the extra light they appreciate.

TEMPERATURE AND SHADING

Cattleyas are among the most easily grown of orchids and will withstand adverse conditions much better than the great majority of other genera. Minimum temperatures of 55° F. at night and 60° F. in daytime are sufficient to ensure a good display of flowers most of the year round, these temperatures being exceeded most of the time through natural warmth. Another 5° F. will, admittedly, add to the flowering prospects in winter time, especially of the yellow hybrids and of the brassavola crosses. The removal of the outdated moisture staging or stage covering is sometimes all that is needed to achieve this temperature increase, as I have proved to my own satisfaction, allowing the heat from the pipes to rise among the plants. As for shading, these plants love all the light and warmth they can get in daytime, short of scorching. The aim should be well-ripened growths of a pale green colour, even

PLATE XLIX. Cypripedium "Chrysostom," var. Stanle
Baldwin × "Harry Thom"

PLATE L
Cypripedium
"Lady Sara"

PLATE LI. Cypripedium "Wirtzianum"

PLATE LII. Cypripedium "Maudiae," Bankhouse var.

PLATE LIII. Cypripedium "Albion"

if they do not look as attractive as the well-shaded, dark green leaved ones. It is a well-known fact that plants suspended from the glazing bars or purlins invariably do better than those growing on a crowded stage. Enhanced aeration may have something to do with it, but whatever the reason, it is well worth trying. Whether "permanent" shading or lath blinds are in use, they should only be applied during the summer months, to prevent scorching of the leaves. A roof-lining of Windolite or Polythene is all that is needed for eight out of twelve months. Spraying of the plants will greatly increase the danger of scorch and should not, in any case, be practised on adult or flowering-sized plants.

VENTILATION AND ATMOSPHERIC MOISTURE

Ventilate freely in daytime, whenever the weather is warm or mild. In cold weather, especially when chilly winds are blowing, choose the lesser of two evils and keep the ventilators closed. Even on cold winter days the sun often obliges for an hour or two, when it is possible to admit fresh air and to discharge surplus moisture. In the evening, the ventilators should be closed again before the temperature of the house has started to fall and the floor damped down, provided the temperature does not fall below 55° F., otherwise defer the latter operation until warmer weather makes it possible again. In prolonged close conditions there is a real danger of rot setting in on leaves, starting at the tips and sometimes even affecting the pseudo-bulbs. When this happens, cut away affected parts with a sharp knife or scissors and dust the cuts with powdered charcoal. The leaves should be occasionally wiped with a damp cloth to remove dust and grime settled on them.

POTTING MATERIALS AND REPOTTING

Use a rather coarser compost for cattleyas, with two parts of osmunda fibre to one of sphagnum moss as a base. Add one handful of flaked oak leaves or spent hops (hop manure must be washed and freed from fertilizers) per gallon of compost and crock well. Pot firmly but not hard, bearing in mind that cattleyas produce long, thick roots which must have somewhere to go. If the compost is rammed in, instead of gently pressed round the roots, the new roots will find the easier way over the rim of the pot into the wide, open spaces, where they are liable to get damaged.

When division of a plant is carried out, either for the purposes of propagation or the removal of spent back-bulbs, cut through the rhizome only and tear the portions apart. To facilitate separation and preserve the live roots, soak the plant thoroughly before removal from the pot. This soaking will also release the roots adhering to the pot itself. Remove as much of the spent compost as possible without damaging new roots and cut away all dead ones. It is quite in order to cut back live roots to within a few inches of the rhizome if they have grown too long to be accommodated in the new compost without breaking them, as they will branch out again. Roots which have grown over the pot rim are best cut off, as they are certain to snap off if forced into the new compost. Such live roots which have been broken or cut off should be incorporated in the new compost to help in spreading the mycorrhiza (microscopic growth organisms), especially in divisions with no live roots.

Leave at least three bulbs behind the lead or new growth, unless these are too badly shrivelled to be of any use to the plant. The surface compost must be "built up" close to the base of the new growth, so that new roots issuing from it can enter the compost immediately, but without burying the rhizome of the bulbs behind. The rhizomes of some cattleyas, however, have the habit of growing upward instead of forward horizontally, and in such cases it is better to build the surface layer of compost into a mound under the new lead in preference to burying the rhizome of the back-bulbs too deeply. With the "sandwich" method of surfacing described earlier on, this will present no difficulties. Back portions with few or no live roots should be potted in fibre and moss in equal proportions and in moss only in the case of weakly, spindly old growths.

If the right size pot has been chosen, there should be sufficient space for two new growths before the new lead reaches the edge of the pot. A cattleya can make two successive growths the same year and will, therefore, be in need of a "shift" into a larger pot after twelve months, unless this space can be created in the same pot by the removal of at least two back-bulbs. If it produces only one new bulb per year, the pot chosen should be just big enough to accommodate two new bulbs, requiring a "shift" every second year. The rhizomes of some varieties extend much farther than they do in others and it is therefore quite impossible to say whether repotting should be carried out annually or biennially. It is mostly a matter of space, depending on the plant's future development, and each plant must be considered on its own merit. It is bad practice to allow the bulbs to grow over the rim of the pot, or so close that the new roots are bound to miss the compost. If oval pots were available, these would make ideal receptacles for cattleya plants, as they usually develop in one direction only. As it is, we have to use round pots and take great care not to allow too great a volume of compost per plant, otherwise correct watering becomes a work of art. There are, however, two methods whereby the volume of compost can be reduced, while allowing sufficient surface space for the development of two new growths. One is by using pans or three-quarter pots, and the other by crocking. I do not recommend the method used by a friend of mine, who put whole bricks into the pots. Lifting by weight, to ascertain the moisture content in the compost, went by the board in these cases. Large crocks stood on end, leaving cavities between, serve the purpose better and add very little to the weight of the pot.

The best time for repotting is when new root activity becomes apparent after flowering. This again varies from plant to plant and the amateur cannot do better than to look out for the tips of the roots to emerge from the base of the newer growths. Fortunately cattleyas present two such opportunities every year, but if one is missed, a sharp look-out should be held for the second chance.

WATERING

The cattleyas are epiphytes—*i.e.*, growing on the branches of trees, with most of their roots exposed and therefore subject to alternate wet and dry conditions. Under cultivation the roots are confined in a more or less tight, cramped position, where they do not get the benefit of drying air after each soaking, as they do in their natural state. Much can be done, however, by way of potting and judicious watering to make them feel "at home" in a clay pot. Most of the plants grown today are acclimatized to pot culture and confined atmospheric conditions. If such a plant "goes wrong," it is almost a forgone conclusion that it has been grown too wet for too long a period.

Adult (*i.e.* flowered) plants should be allowed to dry out between each application of water. During their growing period, and especially during the summer months, it is better to dip the plants to ensure thorough wetting of the whole of the compost. Never water a cattleya during a cold spell, unless a minimum temperature of 60° F. can be maintained in the house. No harm will come to the plant if it is starved of root moisture while low temperature readings prevail. In such conditions growth and root action are, at least temporarily, suspended and a wet compost may result in rotting of the roots. Our winter climate being as unpredictable as our summer weather, the amateur is advised to water his plants by can instead of immersion, pouring the water carefully, close to the rim, thus keeping the centre of the compost fairly dry during the cold winter months. This particularly applies to autumn-flowering plants, which enjoy a more or less prolonged winter nap.

Species and primary hybrids are more subject to these resting periods than home-raised and thoroughly acclimatized hybrids. The plants themselves give an indication of dormancy by clouding over the emerald tips of the roots with a white protective skin. New roots, or the reappearance of these emerald tips, indicate that the plant has started growing again and that it is in need of regular water supplies. Some cattleyas, especially those grown "warm," will produce secondary growths, generally referred to as "winter growths." Do not, however, let these "winter growths" deceive you into watering their hosts, unless their appearance is accompanied by root action. A vigorous plant is capable of producing a complete growth out of its stored reserves, and I repeat that the roots—and not the growths—must be the determining factor for watering.

Unflowered seedling plants must be kept going unchecked and watered all the year round. They require slightly more warmth than the minimum recommended for adult plants. The same applies to divisions and back propagations which should, however, only be "dewed" over with a fine spray, when the temperature is well above the minimum, until new roots appear. It is useless and detrimental watering such rootless pieces.

PLANTS IN BUD AND FLOWER

Far too often one comes across a head of deformed cattleya blooms, because they have got into one another's way and were thus prevented from expanding in a normal way. This need not be, and can easily be prevented by a little foresight and ingenuity. The steps necessary to prevent "crowding" of the blooms must be taken while they are in the bud stage—*i.e.,* when the individual stems are long enough to draw the buds away from their neighbours. In the first place the plants should be positioned in such a way as to cause the light to draw the buds away from obstructing leaves. Complications can then only arise if the plant bears three or four flowers, which may call for two or three separate stakes placed in such positions as to enable the buds to be drawn in different directions, with the help of thin ties. Any bloom that refuses to be drawn into an upright position should have a separate stake with a slit, clamped on the stem, so that the flower can be turned into an upright position. All cattleya blooms should be tied into a slightly reclining position to induce the heavy petals to fall backwards, rather than forward towards the lip. A little trouble taken in correct staking will make all the difference in the display of cattleya blooms.

Keeping the flowers well shaded and cool may prolong the display considerably. Do not, however, transfer plants in flower into a house where the temperature drops to below 50° F., as the blooms may get covered with black spots. If you leave the flowers on the plants for a fortnight and then put them in a vase, they will decorate the living room for a few more days.

In certain parts of the country, including mine, fog and smog play havoc with cattleya blooms and even with unopened buds. An effective preventive lies in placing saucers filled with ammonia on the floor of the cattleya house, whenever fog is anticipated.

14

MILTONIA

WHAT a magnificent show of colourful giant blooms, a few diminutive miltonia plants in flower can provide—at a time when the flowering season of the other main groups of orchids has come to an end! The flat, open, pansy-like blooms are unlike any other orchid flower, and their graceful bearing on slender, arching spikes should make them "hot" favourites with amateurs with an eye for floral beauties. The stems, bearing up to seven flowers, grow up straight from the bracts of the lower leaves, but become bowed by sheer weight of the large blooms. The plants themselves present an attractive appearance by their fan-like, pale-green leaves and oval, flattish pseudo-bulbs. The bulb of some varieties may produce two spikes simultaneously, to be followed by a third, after cutting the first two. The main flowering season is from April to June, but individual plants will be found to flower during the winter months. Utterly devoid of vices, miltonias are among the least difficult orchids to grow, if their principal cultural requirements are understood.

Why is it then that so many amateurs fail to cultivate these plants successfully? The answer must be sought in the erroneous notions which somehow seem to have attached themselves to the culture of miltonias. These plants make little growth during the summer months, when they should be grown as cool as possible and well shaded. They also appreciate a fair amount of fresh air. Close conditions will induce basal rot and leaf fungus disease. In the autumn the growth starts to quicken at an ever-increasing crescendo, when warmth is called for, coupled with a decrease in shading. Provided miltonias get sufficient atmospheric moisture when the leaves can cope with it, that is at night and early morning, they need very little root moisture—at all times. Their tender roots soon rot off if kept constantly moist, and that is where the trouble usually starts.

I prefer to dip miltonias up to three-quarters of the pot's depth, thus keeping the surface compost dry for most of the time. If the new roots find moisture on the surface, they seldom penetrate the compost to any appreciable depth, but are liable to rot off before they have gained much in length. The potting compost should consist of half osmunda fibre and half sphagnum moss, chopped up finely. Potting must not be hard—only firm enough to hold the plant steady and to prevent cavities. Choose the pans or pots on the small side, the latter well-crocked, to ensure rapid disposal of surplus moisture. The compost must never be allowed to become soggy or sour. Once that happens, repotting in fresh compost is the only answer to the danger of decay. Annual repotting of miltonias is advisable and can take place at any time after flowering, but should be discontinued after September. Do not water after repotting until new root action becomes evident.

Never "crowd" the miltonias, otherwise they will lose their attractive appearance, the leaves being forced out of their fan-shaped, arching fashion, to become broken, drooping appendixes. My miltonias are housed in the cypripedium section, which seems to provide just the right conditions for these lovely orchids. Not that I would not like to grow them in a house by themselves, but lack of space leaves me no alternative.

Once the flower spikes appear, the roots have got hold of the compost and more frequent inspection for watering should be made. Also, the temperature should not be allowed to drop below 60° F. in daytime. At night, the miltonias are satisfied with a minimum temperature of 55° F. Unless a number of flowers are carried by a spike, staking is only required to train it in the direction desired and to ensure an unobstructed display of the blooms. Kept well-shaded and cool, the flowers will last up to a month on the plants, or two weeks in water. They are unsuitable for the cut-flower market as they will collapse within the hour of cutting, unless kept in water.

Miltonia Species

CANDIDA. A Brazilian species with yellowish tint and red-brown blotches. The lip is white with a purple-blotched centre. Rather small, compared with the Colombian species and modern hybrids. Autumn flowering.

CLOWESII. From Brazil, similar to the preceding species in size and habit, but of darker colouring.

ROEZLII. From Colombia, the flowers are larger, about 4 inches across and of better shape than the Brazilian species. The sepals and petals are white, with a purple base. The lip is large, bilobed, yellow at the base. A good parent for hybridizing. Usually flowers in the early spring.

SCHRŒDERIANA. From Costa Rica, now rare, fragrant and free-flowering. The sepals and petals are of a bright red-brown with yellow tips. The lip is rosy purple and white, of pleasing shape. Winter flowering.

SPECTABILIS. From Brazil. A spectacular species, as the name implies, with large white or creamy-white sepals and petals, tinged purple at the base. The large bilobed lip is white, with bright purple blotches and yellow crest. The flowers are carried singly on short, numerous stems. Very variable and autumn flowering.

VEXILLARIA. From Colombia. Very variable in colouring, but of good shape and size and very free-flowering; all desirable attributes which have been carried down a long string of hybrids. The spikes are up to 18 inches long, usually carrying five to seven large flowers. Three and sometimes four spikes on a single bulb is by no means unusual in this grand and useful species. The flowers are rose or purple coloured, with yellow lines radiating from the white mask at the apex of the large, bilobed lip. Spring flowering.

PLATE LIV

Cattleya
"Bow Bells"

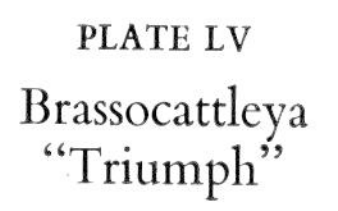

PLATE LV

Brassocattleya
"Triumph"

PLATE LVI

Cattleya
"Bob Betts"

PLATE LVII
Laeliocattleya "Elissa"

PLATE LVIII
Brassocattleya "Marie Marie"

PLATE LIX
Brassolaeliocattleya "Crusader"

PLATE LX. Miltonia "Gattonensis"

PLATE LXI.
Miltonia "Sonnet"

PLATE LXII. Miltonia Hybrids

PLATE LXIII. Miltonia "Lycaena," Stamperland var.

15

ONCIDIUM

THIS genus is studded with interesting species, which show Nature's way of mimicking the animal and insect worlds in a fascinating and life-like manner. Following close on the trail of fanciful reminiscences, there is the graceful ballerina, shapes of diminutive fairies and colourful butterflies, more evident in some than in others, but present in all. A bright-yellow colour, often lacking in other genera, will surely tip the scales in favour of a few oncidium species in any collection of orchids. Although hybrid oncidiums have been raised under cultivation, there can be no question of any preference over the species, which still hold the fort, and may do so for a long time to come, some of the most interesting having refused to hybridize.

The oncidium tribe is a very varied one, growing throughout the South American continent, up to the West Indies and the southern shores of the North American continent, at vastly differing altitudes. Thus some of the species will be at home in the cymbidium house, whilst others require warmer than cattleya house treatment. The great majority of oncidium species will succeed in a mixed collection, providing an extensive choice of varieties. Many oncidium species produce long, branching spikes with numerous flowers, straight, arching or pendant; others have single, but larger, flowers at the tip of the spikes. The floriferousness of some varieties is such as to overtax the strength of the plants which fail to flower altogether the following year, or to produce smaller pseudo-bulbs which should not, in any case, be allowed to flower.

Where the choice exists, the cattleya house is ideally suited for oncidiums, providing more light to ripen their growths for the next flowering effort. They invariably do better when suspended from the roof, or placed on a high shelf, which positions are not always possible to provide, especially for the long-leaved varieties. The amateur should select his plants with great care, according to the accommodation available, for some oncidiums are rampant growers and may soon outstrip their welcome. Others produce such long flower spikes that the owner of a small or low-roofed house may find it difficult to know what to do with the spikes. Tying them into a cartwheel may provide an answer in some instances, but does not do justice to the flowers in others.

The compost should contain, in addition to two parts of osmunda fibre to one of sphagnum moss, a fair proportion of flaked oak leaves or clean tan bark. Never overpot oncidiums, using as small a receptacle as will accommodate the roots, and pot firmly. Allow the plants to dry out between waterings and withhold water altogether when not in active growth. Shrivelling of oncidium bulbs is natural, in view of their gigantic efforts, and any attempt to "fill up" the pseudo-bulbs will only result in over-watering.

For those who would like to grow the striking "butterfly" oncidiums *Papilio* and *Kramerii* and have not sufficient heat at their command, I give a simple dodge that can provide them with the charm of their blooms during any but the cold winter months. These plants will develop quite satisfactorily up to the bud stage in a moderate temperature. If a bud develops to flower during the months of December, January or February, I pinch that bud out, as an insufficient day temperature will only result in a small, deformed flower. Two to three months later, the follow-on bud will find sufficient natural warmth and light to expand in a full-sized, delightful flower, and so on until the following winter.

Oncidium Species

AMPLIATUM. Found in Costa Rica and Nicaragua. The graceful panicles of bright yellow flowers are carried on long, branched stems, bowed by the weight of its numerous flowers. The expanding, bilobed, clear yellow lip is exceptionally large in comparison with the other segments. The small yellow sepals and petals are spotted red-brown at the base.

CAVENDISHIANUM. A native of Guatemala, this remarkable "double-decker" oncidium is one of the finest in existence. Fragrant and bright yellow, the flowers are nearly 2 inches across, numerous, carried on a stout, branching stem up to 3 feet in length. The lip is in two sections, one above the other. The plant has no pseudo-bulbs, but the 2 feet long, 6 inches broad, thick and fleshy leaves, of dark green colour, are well equipped for storing moisture. It is one of the warmer-growing kinds and the cattleya house is indicated. The plants present an unusually attractive appearance, even when out of flower.

CHEIROPHORUM. A dwarf species from Colombia. The panicles of small, yellow, fragrant flowers are carried above the short leaves in arching fashion on a much-branched stem. A very charming, free-flowering species that requires very little overhead room. Ideal for a mixed collection.

CONCOLOR. Another small species, from Brazil, producing pendant spikes with several bright yellow flowers 2 inches across. For the mixed collection.

CRISPUM. A very interesting oncidium, on account of its quaintly shaped flowers. The narrow sepals and broad, rounded petals are brown-olive and narrowed down at the base. The lip is spreading, brown-olive with a clear yellow central blotch, red-brown at the base, as are the side lobes.

EXCAVATUM. From Peru, a good grower with long, branching spikes, carrying numerous medium-sized, bright yellow flowers with brown markings. For the mixed collection.

FLEXUOSUM. Another useful species for the mixed collection, being a small-sized, free-flowering plant, with panicles of small, dainty flowers, looking for all the world like graceful ballerinas; carried on long stems. The narrow sepals and petals are yellow, barred brown, and the prominent lip is yellow with a few red spots. A native of Brazil.

FORBESII. This charming, diminutive species may produce spikes up to 3 feet in length, carrying large, chestnut-brown flowers. The dorsal sepal is barred yellow and the petals are margined yellow, as is the lip. From the Organ Mountains.

INCURVUM. This is an easily grown species from Mexico, for the cool section or mixed collection. The flower spikes never seem to stop growing, branching out in all directions on the entire length of the stem and best managed by tying into a "cartwheel." Over a hundred small, rosy-purple and white flowers are carried in panicles, even on a small-sized plant. The variety *Album* is particularly dainty and attractive.

KRAMERIANUM. A spectacular species of the butterfly type that requires a fair amount of heat to flower well. Totally different to the other oncidium species, except *O. Papilio,* it has thick green leaves with brown mottling, and the noded, erect stem carries a single flower, with buds forming in succession as each flower is cut. The flowers do not last long—a fortnight at the most—but present a striking spectacle, with their reddish-brown antennæ-like petals and dorsal sepal, which are undulated along the edges. The lateral sepals are much broader, undulating, semicircular in shape, hugging the lip, and of chocolate-brown and yellow colouring. The large, rounded lip has ruffled margins with brown markings and a bright yellow central area.

LANCEANUM. The plants of this species from British Guiana are similar to *O. Cavendishianum,* but not the flowers. Devoid of pseudo-bulbs, this species relies on its large, leathery, thick leaves for moisture storage. These can reach a length of 2 feet and 8 inches in width and are, therefore, too extravagant in size for restricted spaces. The attractive appeal of the plant is well matched by its large, fragrant yellow, red-brown and purple flowers—quite a striking, tempting combination.

LEUCOCHILUM. Develops large pseudo-bulbs 6 inches high and slender dark-green leaves a foot to 18 inches long. Easily grown with cymbidiums, or in a mixed collection. A single branched spike, 3 to 4 feet long, can produce up to 100 fragrant flowers 1½ inches across. The sepals and petals are uniform, radiating symmetrically from the centre, the yellow tips pleasingly recurved; colour chestnut-brown with irregular streaks of yellow. The bilobed lip is white, spreading and undulating, with lilac suffusion in its narrowed apex, from which are protruding five horns. Column white on top, yellow underneath, with two tiny side lobes of lilac colour, surmounted by a brownish-purple pollen cap. A very dainty shape and colour combination.

MARSHALLIANUM. This species from the Organ Mountains grows best in the cattleya house, but will succeed near the roof, in a mixed collection, where it can find sufficient light. A small plant with only two pseudo-bulbs can provide an astonishing display of bright yellow flowers 2 inches across, carried on a 2 feet long branching stem, in large numbers. The flowers have a habit of reaching for the light, growing horizontally above the stems in panicles as if to provide an umbrella for the plant itself. A "must" for any amateur with at least a moderate amount of heat at his command.

ORNITHORHYNCHUM. Another little gem for the mixed collection, that requires little space or heat. Numerous small, rose-purple flowers are carried in panicles on arching, branched spikes. A native of Mexico.

PAPILIO. Similar to *Oncidium Kramerianum* in its habits, requirements and shape of butterfly-like flowers. Its spikes are longer, more slender, up to 3 feet in length, which sometimes branch, producing single flowers at the end of each branch, in succession, as each flower is cut. The brown markings are of a lighter shade and the lateral sepals are barred, instead of spotted. The antennæ are straight-edged and longer.

SPHACELATUM. A rampant grower from the West Indies, with 6-inch long pseudo-bulbs and long, stiff leaves, it can be grown with cymbidiums or in a mixed collection. The yard-long branched spikes are produced freely and the numerous bright-yellow flowers, sparsely spotted brown, about 1½ inches across, have a somewhat delicate appearance above the large robust plants.

TIGRINUM. A most impressive species from Mexico, which likes light and warmth and is, therefore, best housed with the cattleyas. Does not readily grow into large plants under cultivation and takes a long rest after flowering. To flower this species, however, is well worth any amount of effort, the comparatively large flowers of striking colouring being an imposing sight about 20 inches above a diminutive plant. The recurved sepals and petals are a glossy brown, with irregular bright-yellow streaks across contrasting most effectively with the large bright-yellow lip.

VARICOSUM. Vying with *Oncidium Marshallianum*, but with smaller if more numerous flowers, this species from Brazil has achieved remarkable popularity. Small wonder, in view of its ease of cultivation, modest requirements in heat and space, coupled with the beautiful sight of a hundred or so 1½-inch canary-yellow flowers of long-lasting quality. It is "at home" in the cymbidium house or in a mixed collection, and the sprays of its dainty rich yellow flowers, carried on tall arching and branched spikes, will delight any visitor to the orchid house.

16

DENDROBIUM

One of the largest genera of the orchid family, this epiphytic orchid has a very wide geographical distribution, stretching from India through the East Asiatic countries down to Australia. The diversity of climatic conditions under which they grow in their natural surroundings makes this genus one of the most variable, both in respect of their cultural habits and diversity of colour and flower formation. There are two main groups to be considered for cultural purposes—viz., the Evergreen and the Deciduous Dendrobiums. The former generally produce shorter and harder stems with thicker, tougher leaves than the deciduous dendrobes, the leaves of which grow in pairs on the reed-like growths, which may reach several feet in height. The Evergreens retain their leaves for two or three years, whilst the deciduous type shed theirs as soon as the new growth has ripened—*i.e.*, before flowering.

In no other genus can be found such a wealth of deep golden-yellow colour, apart from white, rose and purple of all shades, nor the tightly packed clusters of flowers hanging down like bunches of grapes. The dendrobiums are singularly free from insect trouble, except perhaps the evergreen *D. fimbriatum*, which is prone to attack from Red Spider mite and must be closely watched for any signs of an attack. Dendrobiums love the light, even direct sun rays, short of scorching the leaves, and grow particularly well appended to a brick wall facing a southerly direction.

Hybrid dendrobiums have been raised in plenty of improved sizes and shapes, but the colours have undergone little change. Who knows what the future holds in this respect? Maybe the dendrobium with the large purple sepals and petals and golden-yellow, fimbriated lip is just round the corner! If such combinations did turn up, I am not so sure whether I should like it any better than, or as much as, the solid gold of the *D. fimbriatum*, *D. chrysotoxum*, or *D. aggregatum* and others.

Most dendrobiums flower in the spring, but will do so all through the winter given sufficient warmth and light. The deciduous type benefit by a decided rest after the appearance of the last two terminal leaves, when water should be given sparingly at monthly intervals. When the flower buds begin to swell on the nodes of the previous year's growths, normal watering should be resumed at more frequent intervals, according to the temperature of the house and prevailing weather conditions. If the plants are allowed to dry out between each application of water, preferably by immersion, they are all the better for it. The evergreen kinds, too, should be watered sparingly when growth has slowed down or stopped, and kept in a day-temperature of not less than 60° F.

My dendrobiums are growing in the cattleya house on and against a high brick wall facing south-west, where they get subdued sunshine even when the blinds are in position. This position has proved to their liking, as evidenced by their generous flowering from January onwards. Considering that they are the "forgotten tribe" of my orchid collection and subject to what almost amounts to neglect, it speaks well for their good nature and flowering propensities. Neither are they particular with regard to the potting medium. I have potted them in osmunda fibre and sphagnum moss only, and with fibrous loam or tan bark added, but have not noticed any difference in growth or their generous flower production.

Firm potting, however, is indicated, the roots being fairly stiff and wiry, of good penetrating substance. The lasting quality of their flowers vary considerably between different species, ranging from one to four weeks, the yellows being the most short-lived and the white *D. Jamesianum* flowers the longest-lived within my ken.

Deciduous dendrobiums often produce adventitious plantlets from the nodes on the stem and these can be gently prised off when the roots are a couple of inches long, and potted up singly or in batches to make large plants in two or three years' time. These potted plantlets should not be watered, but sprayed occasionally when the temperature is well up, otherwise they will quickly rot off. Once the roots have established themselves in the new compost and growth is in evidence, they can be watered in the normal way. Another method of propagation is cutting up the stems that have completed their growth, as well as back growths which are still in good condition and not shrivelled, into short pieces, each with a node, burying them in fresh sphagnum moss but with the nodes exposed. Encouraged by a warm moist atmosphere, new growths will eventually appear from the nodes, which can be dealt with in the same way as the nodal growths from the stems. A third method of propagation is that adopted with pseudo-bulbous plants, viz., by division of the plant, which is the procedure most frequently practised for the evergreen dendrobiums.

Dendrobium Species

AGGREGATUM. A Burmese species with short, wrinkled, single-leaved stems and short leathery leaves. Flowers golden-yellow with orange lip, in pendant bunches of a dozen or so flowers. For the cattleya house.

ATRO-VIOLACEUM. This distinct species from New Guinea is, unfortunately, rare in cultivation. It has foot-long clavate stems, bearing up to a dozen pendant white flowers, richly spotted violet-mauve, with a violet-coloured lip. The flower buds, attractive in themselves with their violet-mauve spotting, take several weeks to open and the flowers are exceptionally long lasting. Best grown with cattleyas.

AUREUM. Found in India, Burma and the Philippines, with fragrant 2-inch amber-yellow flowers, issuing from the nodes—in pairs, or threes on 12- to 18-inch stems. The lip is of a brighter yellow with purple streaks.

BIGGIBUM. An Australian species, with bright magenta-purple, rounded 2-inch flowers with a darker lip. Flowers long lasting, produced in clusters from the top of 18-inch stems.

BRYMERIANUM. From Burma. Golden-yellow flowers, 3 inches across, growing in twos and threes on the upper half of the stem, up to 2 feet tall. The lip is large and beautifully fringed, which makes this one of the most attractive species.

CHRYSOTOXUM. An easily grown Burmese species of modest size, which can be grown in a mixed collection near the roof. The pendant tightly-packed bunches of numerous golden-yellow flowers never fail to attract the admiration of visitors to the

PLATE LXIV

Dendrobium
"Virginale," Orchidhurst var.

PLATE LXV

Dendrobium
"Chrysotoxum"

PLATE LXVI (*left*)
Brassia "Brachiata"

PLATE LXVII (*below*)
Brassavola "Digbyana"

orchid house. The lip is orange-yellow, richly and beautifully fringed.

DEAREI. A white-flowered species from the Philippines, the 3-inch flowers growing in clusters from the top of the yard-long stems.

DENSIFLORUM. From Nepal, with club-shaped 15-inch stems, bearing 6-inch long leathery leaves. Loves light and warmth and produces tightly packed bunches of bright-yellow flowers with frilled orange-yellow lip.

FIMBRIATUM. Another gem from Nepal, but growing to 4 feet and over. The golden-yellow flowers with beautifully fringed lip hang in clusters of a dozen or more from the end of the drooping stems. A well-flowered specimen plant presents a sight not easily forgotten. The variety *Oculatum* is more often met with than the type and has a striking maroon spot in the centre of the fringed lip.

FORMOSUM. A fine white species from Burma. Clusters of three to five chaste white 4-inch flowers top the stout hairy stems, which grow from 12 to 18 inches tall. The white broad lip has a large orange blotch in the centre. The variety *Giganteum* has even larger flowers and is more popular than the type.

INFUNDIBULUM. Similar to *D. formosum*, the variety *Jamesianum* is better known in this country than the type. From Burma, it produces paper-white, glistening, flat and well-rounded flowers 3½ inches across, sometimes ten to a cluster at the apex of the stiff, dark-coloured, hairy 18-inch stem. Can be grown in a light position in a mixed collection. The lip has an orange-red blotch in the centre.

NOBILE. This very popular and variable species from India is a rampant grower, quickly developing into fine specimen plants up to 2 feet in height. Suitable for a mixed collection. The petals and sepals are white, with rose-purple near the tips. The lip is rounded, white, with a deep purple blotch in the throat. The flowers are about 3 inches across and the colouring varies according to the variety.

PHALÆNOPSIS. This aristocrat of the dendrobium tribe hails from Australia and requires a fair amount of heat to flower well. The beautiful shape of the 3-inch flowers is well matched by their colouring, which ranges from rose to dark purple. The sepals are usually of a rosy purple shade, the petals mauve, attractively veined with a deeper colour and the lip maroon-purple, the colours varying in shades according to the many varieties.

SUPERBIENS. Another Australian species, growing up to 4 feet in height, with apical clusters of crimson-purple, 2-inch flowers. The lip has distinct white raised lines radiating from the throat, contrasting with their dark purple background.

SUPERBUM. From the Philippines, growing up to 4 feet high, the numerous fragrant flowers issue in pairs from the nodes along the stem and measure up to 5 inches across. The sepals and petals are of a magenta-rose and the furrowed lip is wine-red.

THYRSIFLORUM. From Burma, similar to *D. densiflorum* but with white sepals and petals and broad orange-yellow lip. May produce thirty or more 2-inch flowers on both old and new growths.

WARDIANUM. This Burmese species is a very charming one, but has proved disappointing under cultivation in this country. The flowers are of good, lasting substance, 3 inches across, growing in twos and threes along the length of the stem. The sepals and petals are white, tipped magenta, and the lip spreading, white, yellow in the throat, with two maroon blotches.

17

MISCELLANEOUS ORCHIDS

SO FAR I have dealt with the main groups of orchids, each one being capable of providing sufficient variation in material to form large collections, without contributions from other genera. A further selection from other tribes is made in the following pages for the amateur with a flair for an even more varied collection. Some of these tribes are large enough to form collections of their own, especially with the help of numerous hybrids, whilst many more genera must needs be left out altogether.

Bearing in mind that most amateurs cultivate mixed collections, comprising a number of genera, the following selection of tribes include interesting and, for the most part, easily grown plants. Their cultural requirements should be studied before deciding on the inclusion of one or other of the genera cited, in order to avoid disappointments arising from a wrong combination. It is thus useless trying to grow a brassavola or phalænopsis, if the bulk of the collection consists of cymbidiums, unless separate growing facilities are available. It would be equally foolhardy cluttering up valuable space in a small house with tall-growing epidendrums, for instance, when there are so many small-growing types to choose from which produce much showier flowers. Unless otherwise stated, the genera listed hereafter are epiphytic.

Bifrenaria

The popular variety *Harrisoniæ* produces waxy, glistening-white flowers, about 3 inches across, of a beautiful upstanding shape, which last a long time on the plant. The broad rounded sepals and petals are about equal in size and the erect lip is hairy, deep purple, with vividly contrasting white column. Yellow and purple colours are found in other varieties, unfortunately rare in this country. The pseudo-bulbs and broad leathery leaves grow to a height of approximately 1 foot. A good grower for the mixed collection, which thrives on cypripedium compost but likes more light. A native of Brazil.

Brassavola

One of the parents of the bigeneric brassocattleya, found in Brazil and the West Indies, this species should only be attempted in a light, warm house where the minimum temperature can be kept above 60° F. With its beautifully and prominently frilled lip, the *Brassavola* var. *Digbyana* is fragrant and one of the showiest members of the orchid family. The colour of the enormous fringed lip is of a greenish white, darker green in the lower centre, column white and the sepals and petals about equal in size, greenish, straight but narrow. Compost and potting as for cattleyas. The plant is small, slow-growing, the pseudo-bulbs slender, erect, as are the stiff, thick, pale-green leaves, attractively covered in a farina-like secretion.

Brassia

Often referred to as the Spider orchid because of its spidery shape. This genus has a wide distribution, ranging from Mexico to the south of Brazil. Of easy culture, ideal for the mixed collection. For sheer exotic, arresting appearance, one or two of the species should be included in every collection. Compost as for cypripediums.

BRACHIATA. The long, narrow, straight sepals and petals are green. spotted purple-brown towards the centre. The lower sepals reach 6 to 7 inches in length. The recurved lip is creamy white spotted olive-green on the reflexed upper half. The 2-feet-long flower spike carries seven or eight flowers. The rhizomes extend upwards, necessitating annual repotting to keep the pseudo-bulbs at pot level.

LAWRENCEANA. The flowers of this species are bright yellow, greenish towards the centre, with red-brown spots. The sepals are longer, narrower than in *B. brachiata* and somewhat stringy.

VERRUCOSA. This is a fast grower and, unlike the two preceding species, the rhizomes of the pseudo-bulbs extend horizontally, which makes it possible to grow large specimen plants. A small plant which had one bulb and two leads when I acquired it, grew into a fine specimen plant, bearing eighteen flower spikes a yard long, with 216 blooms—an average of twelve blooms each—all in a matter of four years. Such a plant almost needs a greenhouse on its own when in flower, the spikes arching out in all directions, giving a total reach of 7 feet. For this reason this fine plant had to be disposed of the following year, when it had seventy to eighty leading growths. The flowers are of a lighter colour than those of *B. brachiata*, otherwise very similar.

Cochlioda

This species, and the variety *Noezliana* in particular, is one of the famous parents that have given birth to the bigeneric odontioda, when crossed with members of the odontoglossum tribe; to the miltonioda, when crossed with miltonias; and to the oncidioda, when crossed with oncidiums. It is also a contributory partner in trigeneric and quadrigeneric hybrids, such as vuylstekeara and burrageara. Its most valuable contribution lies in the brilliant orange-scarlet colouring of the *cochlioda* var. *Noezliana*, which it has freely imparted to its multigeneric offspring. The small size of its flowers, about 1½ inches across, is well compensated by its brilliant scarlet colouring and its well-furnished arching spikes. *C. Noezliana* was discovered in Northern Peru, a diminutive plant, which deserves a place in the odontoglossum house or the mixed collection.

Cœlogyne

A large family of greatly differing forms and colours, distributed over a wide area in East Asia. Only a comparatively few species are found in general cultivation, probably more for considerations of space and the high temperatures some require, than attractiveness of the flowers. The few species given below are epiphytic and showy, but with one exception require rather high temperatures to grow well and are somewhat extravagant in their requirements for space.

MASSANGEANA. From the Malayan Peninsula, it has 4-inch ovate pseudo-bulbs and broad leaves up to 18 inches long. The pendulous racemes of creamy-white and brown 2-inch flowers may reach a length of 2 to 3 feet. It should be cultivated in baskets suspended from the roof of the cypripedium house, if sufficient overhead space exists.

MOOREANA. A moderate-sized species from Assam, it can be

grown either with odontoglossums or in a mixed collection. It requires copious supplies of water when in growth, but hates overpotting. A moisture-retentive rooting medium consisting of equal proportions of fibre and moss, with some flaked oak leaves added, will suit this species. The flowers, usually five to seven on erect spikes, are of a shimmering white, with a bright yellow throat. The variety *Brockhurst* has larger flowers, about 3 inches across, and its sepals and petals are broader.

PANDURATA. A native of Borneo, it is not a proposition for the small house, its leaves growing to 2 feet in length on top of 6-inch pseudo-bulbs, and the long spikes grow out almost horizontally. The rhizome extends several inches, calling for large, oblong baskets to accommodate the plant and to ensure maximum possible root aeration. The compost should consist of two parts of sphagnum moss to one of osmunda fibre, with plenty of broken crocks worked in. The flowers, however, are of such striking colouring as to tempt many to acquire this species—and rightly so, provided sufficient space and heat are available. The sepals and petals are emerald-green; the large lip is prominently veined and blotched with black on a greenish background and garnished with a fringed central lobe and black warts.

TOMENTOSA. Found in Borneo and Sumatra, this is another species that revels in moist heat. The pseudo-bulbs are 5 inches high and the broad, plicate leaves 18 inches long. About eighteen small orange-red flowers cluster tightly in a pendulous spray. A plant placed on a high shelf in my cypripedium house has proved itself a very fast grower and free flowerer.

Epidendrum

This is another genus that offers an almost inexhaustible choice in the vast number of species and varieties found on two continents—viz., the southern part of the U.S.A. and South America, as well as in Central America. Like the large cœlogyne tribe, the genus epidendrum has not found as much favour in our collections as have some of the much smaller members of the orchid family. Apart from a few "gems," epidendrums have had to concede too much ground to their showier relatives to warrant more than a few scanty references in this book. If we in this country were blessed with the climate of their ancestral homes,

I should not hesitate to plant a hedge of epidendrums in my garden, but, placed as we are, they have to be grown under glass and compete with their showier cousins. The more's the pity as they readily intercross with members of other genera and are generally of easy culture. Owing to the wide geographical distribution of the genus epidendrum, cultural requirements vary considerably, but most will be found to grow quite well in a mixed collection. A compost of two parts of osmunda fibre to one part of sphagnum moss suits most epidendrums. The following species have much to commend themselves and could form a basis for a selection.

ATROPURPUREUM. A small species from Mexico, producing eight to ten comparatively large flowers on an arching stem from the top of the roundish pseudo-bulbs. The sepals and petals are curving inwardly and are of brown and green colour, the spreading lip white with crimson stripes. A very charming, long-lasting flower.

COCHLEATUM. Another small species distributed over Central America, the flowers are 3 inches across, grown in clusters of six or seven on top of the erect stem. The sepals and petals are curved at the tips, yellow-green, the lip white striped purple.

FRAGRANS. Found in the West Indies and northern Brazil, producing clusters of three to five 2-inch fragrant flowers, upside-down. Colour creamy-white with purple stripes on the lip.

RADICANS. A tall-growing species from Guatemala, often used for hybridizing; for the cattleya house, but grown against a wall where the 4 to 5 feet stems can be secured. Produces many aerial roots along the length of the stems, as well as little plantlets, which can be removed and potted separately. The 2-inch flowers are borne in clusters, cinnabar-red, with fringed lip.

VITELLINUM. From Mexico, its variety *majus* is a popular species. Can be grown in the cymbidium or odontoglossum house. Of vivid cinnabar-red and yellow colouring, the small flowers are produced in sprays of ten to fifteen on erect stems.

Hæmaria

I have a very soft spot for this lowly, diminutive terrestrial orchid and have yet to find someone who does not share my admiration for the sheer beauty of this velvety, soft-coloured, golden-veined "Jewel Orchid." Granted that the flowers are hardly worth the particular care and attention required by this tribe under cultivation, the artistry and colouring Mother Nature has employed in designing its semi-lucent leaves more than make up for the shortcomings of the flowers.

Of tropical origin, the "Jewel Orchid" requires more warmth than can generally be provided in an amateur's small greenhouse. This need not, however, deprive anyone of the pleasure of growing these beautiful things. Where a cypripedium house temperature and atmospheric conditions are not available, a bell glass will usually do the trick. As long as the bell glass is at least partly lifted in daytime for short periods, the extra warmth and confined moisture will in most cases make their cultivation possible. With this aid many a living room can be adorned by their presence. A propagating frame, such as used for starting back-bulbs into growth, or a Wardian case, are eminently suited for the cultivation of these beautiful orchid plants. For once you do not have to wait for the result of your efforts, the "Jewel Orchid" is at its best all the year round! A shallow pan is the most suitable receptacle, to be filled with chopped sphagnum moss, with a little leaf mould and coarse sand added. As the rhizomes extend they should be pegged down level with the compost surface. Division is effected by cutting through the rhizome. The severed pieces must be kept on the dry side until new roots are formed. The flower spikes should be pinched out, for the benefit of the beautiful colourful leaves.

The Jewel Orchid family has been divided into several genera by the botanists, no doubt for reasons of their own, and the species listed below are sometimes marketed under the group-name of ANOECTOCHILUS.

DAWSONIANA, from Malaya, is particularly fascinating, the velvety, elliptical leaves, reaching 3½ by 2½ inches on maturity, are of a deep-purple colour with an olive-green sheen and shimmering, purple red veining, light-purple on the underside.

DISCOLOR. From the Islands of Singapore to southern China, its velvety leaves are pointed, dark greenish-brown on top, and light-purple on the underside.

ORDIANA, has olive-green leaves with silver veining.

RUBROVENIA, has velvety, bronze-green leaves with copper-red veins.

SIKKIMENSIS. The leaves are olive-green with shimmering copper-red veining.

ANOECTOCHILUS (more popularly known as MACODES) PETOLA. The brown-olive, velvety leaves are egg-shaped and irregularly patterned with shimmering, emerald-green veins—unquestionably the most beautiful of the Jewel Orchid family.

Lælia

It might be said that the tribe Lælia has killed its former popularity by its own prolific contribution to the showier bigeneric progeny læliocattleya. This combination with members of the cattleya family has given birth to a decidedly superior race of orchids, both in respect of shape and size as well as improvement of colours. Whilst the majority of lælias have thus disappeared from our collections, some of the species have refused to pass on their fragrance or richest colouring to their bigeneric progenies, making sure of their survival.

Resembling the cattleyas in habit and appearance, but generally smaller in size, lælia species are particularly useful to the amateur with a small house, or with insufficient heat for growing cattleyas. Diminutive species of the lælia family can thus provide him with cattleya-like flowers, with strong and varied scents. Some of the species originate from high altitudes and will, therefore, thrive in moderately heated houses, occupying but little space. The compost recommended for cattleyas will suit them, but they take a decided and often prolonged rest, when water should be supplied very sparingly.

Of easy culture, the following species are among the most popular, but their flowering season varies according to the temperature of the house.

ANCEPS. A popular small winter-flowering Mexican species, which produces jointed flower spikes from 12 to 18 inches long, arched by the weight of three to four terminal 4-inch flowers. Sepals and petals rather narrow, of rosy-purple colour, the infolded lip deep purple, with yellow and purple veined throat. There are several varieties, ranging from white to dark purple colouring.

AUTUMNALIS. Another small but popular species from Mexico, closely resembling *Lælia anceps*, the 18- to 24-inch spikes usually carry five to six 4-inch flowers of a bright rosy-purple colour, with a more open and broader lip than *L. anceps*. The fragrant flowers are produced in the autumn, as the name suggests.

CINNABARINA. A spring-flowering Brazilian species with attractive cinnabar-red flowers 3 inches across, half a dozen or more in number opening in succession.

FLAVA. A dwarf autumn-flowering species from Brazil, with small but bright-yellow flowers, carried in clusters on a foot-long stem. Popular with hybridists on account of its rich yellow colour.

GOULDIANA. A reputed natural hybrid between *L. autumnalis* and *L. anceps*. Flowering usually around Christmas, its soft, velvety, fragrant, mauve-purple flowers are 4 inches across, of good shape and long-lasting quality, three to four in number on 16- to 18-inch long erect items.

PUMILA. Another dwarf species, introduced from British Guiana, producing single rosy-purple 4-inch flowers. The lip is crimson-purple, yellow in the throat with ruffled middle lobe.

PURPURATA. The largest of the lælia family, producing three to four large flowers on stout pseudo-bulbs up to 20 inches high. The flowers may reach 7 to 8 inches in diameter and are of a rosy-purple colour, white in the varieties *Schrœderæ* and *alba*, with large crimson-purple lip and yellow lined throat. Should be grown in the cattleya house, where it flowers in the spring. A favourite with hybridizers.

TENEBROSA. This striking spring-flowering species from Brazil has large flowers with orange-yellow to copper-bronze sepals and petals and a crimson-purple lip with a whitish border. The fragrance of its flowers has been imparted to many of its bigeneric hybrids.

Lycaste

The species of this tribe generally originate from high altitudes in Central and South America. They can be grown almost with every tribe, so long as shading is adequate, otherwise the plicate leaves become discoloured and stunted before they have reached maturity. Ideal for the mixed collection, but the long, broad leaves of some varieties require a fair amount of headroom. When the pseudo-bulbs have fully matured, the leaves turn yellow and brown and gradually die off, often before the flowers appear, the leafless plants occupying but little space.

It is a fascinating and showy tribe, producing well-shaped, often fragrant, flowers of white, green, yellow and purple colouring, and they last exceptionally long on the plant if kept cool and well shaded. The lycastes do not object to low temperatures when fully matured and can safely be taken into the living room when in flower.

Although essentially epiphytic, lycastes appreciate a little fibrous loam in their compost of two parts of osmunda fibre to one of sphagnum moss, as well as some flaked oak leaves. They should be kept fairly dry and in a sunny position after flowering, but not to the extent of shrivelling of the bulbs.

Some of the outstanding hybrid crosses of the Lycaste tribe are *L. Balliæ*, of a velvety, deep-purple colour; *L. Brugensis*, creamy white; L. Sir Jeremiah Colman, white; *L. Hera*, yellow; *L. Imschootiana*, greenish-brown; *L. Lucianii*, white and rose; *L. Olivia*, greenish-white; L. Queen Elizabeth, creamy green.

Lycaste Species

AROMATICA. An ideal plant for the amateur with a small house. Several golden-yellow fragrant flowers, about 2 inches across, with a red-dotted lip, emerge from the base of the new pseudo-bulb, on slender 6-inch stems. The deciduous plicate leaves are about 8 to 10 inches long. A native of Mexico.

CRUENTA. From Guatemala, very much like *L. aromatica* but with larger, greenish-yellow flowers, with a red blotch at the base of the lip and leaves from 12 to 15 inches long.

DEPPEI. An attractive species from Guatemala. The sepals are pale green with purplish spots, the petals white and the lip yellow—altogether a charming combination of colours. The leaves are about a foot long, the stems 6 to 8 inches and the flowers 4 inches across.

GIGANTEA. Discovered in Ecuador, this is the largest of the lycaste species, with broad leaves 2 feet long. The olive-green sepals and petals are contrasted by a purple-shaded yellow-edged lip. The flowers are 5 to 6 inches across and carried on erect stems 18 inches long.

LOCUSTA. This is a striking but rare species, which relies on its white column to attract attention. The 3-inch flowers are of a deep green and might easily be overlooked, were it not for the pure white column and the prominently and beautifully fringed lip.

SKINNERI. This is no doubt the most popular of the lycaste species. A strong grower, it freely produces its waxy, white and rose-tinged flowers, from 5 to 6 inches across, on foot-long stems from the base of the last made-up pseudo-bulb. Many varieties, with purple shading of varying intensity, are in cultivation under varietal names, but the most charming of them all is the pure, glistening white *L. Skinneri alba,* although not such a strong grower.

Bigeneric Lycastes

Two strikingly beautiful and distinct races of bigeneric Lycastes have been raised in recent years by Sir William Cooke and his daughter, Miss Betty Cooke, at Wyld Court. The fine, outstanding results obtained from these two crosses, viz. the Lycasteria and Angulocaste go to prove that the field of intergeneric crosses involving the Lycaste tribe harbours great potentialities.

LYCASTERIA DARIUS is the outcome of a cross made between *Lycaste Skinnerii* and *Bifrenaria Harrisoniæ* and is, so far, the only one in existence. Its large, perfectly shaped flowers have taken after the Lycaste parent and are of a creamy-white colour and of good substance, lasting in perfection for weeks on end.

ANGULOCASTE TUDOR is the offshoot of a cross between Lycaste Queen Elizabeth and *Anguloa Clowesii.* Like the Lycasteria, it has taken after the Lycaste parent in shape. The colour, however, is of a pale pinkish green, faintly speckled with fine pink spots. The flowering season of this bigeneric cross spreads over the summer and autumn months.

ANGULOCASTE APOLLO. Unlike the Angulocaste Tudor, this cross between *Anguloa Clowesii* and *Lycaste Imschootiana* has retained the Anguloa (cradle) shape, but the flower segments are more open than is the case with the latter—a decided improvement over the type. The colour ranges from pure white through shades of cream, with and without spots, to the deep golden yellow of the *A. Apollo F.C.C.* variety. The main flowering season of this cross falls in the late spring, but some of its varieties have been known to flower in other seasons.

Both the Angulocaste crosses so far made have produced flowers of exceptionally good substance, lasting for a long time on the plants, which grow to a larger size than either parent and require more headroom.

Masdevallia

This is a large family of epiphytic orchids, originating from Central and South America. Hardly any other tribe of orchids looks less like an orchid than the Masdevallias, and I have no hesitation in stating that I have never been able to enthuse over this tribe. They are more interesting than beautiful, unless viewed through a magnifying glass, for the petals, and often the lip too, are so small as to be hardly discernible. The fused and tailed lower sepals and the horned dorsal sepal and, in some cases, the lovely colours are the main attraction of the flowers, some of which have an insect-like appearance.

Masdevallias are mostly found in humid regions on high ground and will grow in the coolest section. The plants are quite small, the leaves seldom growing over 6 inches in height, but are not so popular today as of yore, despite their modest space requirements. Pseudo-bulbless, they should never be severely dried out and the compost used for hæmarias suits them.

There is a wide choice of species, grotesque or interesting, but a selection is best made on the spot at a nursery, when in flower, to save disappointments. Amateurs who like to give their visitors a surprise might include the *Masdevallia muscosa,* which has a very sensitive lip which closes at the touch and will trap small insects that alight on it. It is about the smallest of orchid plants.

Maxillaria

The genus *Maxillaria* is eminently suited for cultivation in small houses, the most popular of the species requiring but a modest amount of space and warmth. Epiphytic, originating from Central and South America, the following species are among the most interesting and can be grown in an odontoglossum compost, the most suitable receptacles being shallow pans or baskets.

PICTA. From southern Brazil, the flowers are about 1½ inches across, carried singly on 4-inch stems among the 8- to 9-inches-long leaves. The narrow sepals and petals are yellow with brownish-purple markings; the lip white with red spots.

SANDERIANA. Found on the Andes of Ecuador and in Peru, the large flowers, growing on short stems among the broad, 6- to 12-inches-long leaves, are easily the most attractive of the type. The sepals and petals are white, spotted purple at the base and the lip yellow with red markings, cupped, with undulating margins.

SANGUINEA. This attractive little gem has curiously coloured small flowers, carried on short stems among the narrow leaves. The sepals are reddish-brown, margined and tipped with yellow, the petals yellow, spotted crimson. The red lip is tipped creamy-white.

VENUSTA. The large, pretty flowers of this Venezuelan species have pure white sepals and petals and a red-spotted yellowish lip.

Pleione

Growing mostly at high altitudes in northern India, sometimes called Indian crocuses, the species of this tribe require cool treatment and occupy little space. Although the flowers are very charming, delicately coloured and freely produced, the pleiones are more often met with in cool plant and alpine houses than in orchid collections. The cymbidium house is the most suitable abode for these small, cool-growing orchids of the cœlogyne group. The small pseudo-bulbs only last one year, shedding their single leaves as the growths mature, and the plants are, therefore, best repotted annually after flowering, in shallow, well-drained pans in a mixture of fibre and moss, to which a liberal sprinkling of coarse sand should be added. Keep the plants moist until the leaves have fallen, when water should be almost entirely withheld until the flower buds appear from the bases of the new pseudo-bulbs.

LAGENARIA. From the Khasia hills, with elliptical 5- to 6-inch leaves and short-stemmed flowers about 3 inches across. The sepals and petals are rosy lilac; the fringed white or rose-coloured lip has purple-striped margins, yellow towards the base, with crimson markings and fringed at the edges.

PRÆCOX. Another Indian species growing at high altitudes, requiring cool treatment. The sepals and petals are narrow, of a rose-purple shade, and the fringed lip is striped yellow and white, with a yellow throat.

PRICEI. This Formosan species is near-hardy, with flowers 3 inches across, of a delicate lilac-purple and white, with yellow throat.

Promenæa Citrina

This charming, dwarf-growing species from the Brazilian province of Minas Geraes has been pushed around a bit by the botanists since its introduction about 120 years ago. Popularly known as *Promenæa citrina*, it graduated from *Maxillaria xanthina* through *Promenæa xanthina* to *Zygopetalum xanthinum*.

Of easy cultivation, *Promenæa citrina* likes cool, moist conditions in a light position, preferably on a shelf near the roof glass. It develops very rapidly and never seems to rest. An odontoglossum compost suits this fine species, as do the atmospheric conditions and temperature of the odontoglossum house. The variety Brockhurst has larger flowers than the type, about 1½ inches across, carried singly on 3-inch stems, the soft, narrow leaves being a trifle longer. A dozen or so of its dainty, bright-yellow flowers crowning the numerous pale green leaves is a very attractive sight.

Promenæa Crawshayana has larger flowers with numerous dark pinpoint spots and is a worthy companion to *Promenæa citrina*.

Sophronitis

The bright scarlet-red of the *Sophronitis grandiflora* has been taken advantage of in crossing not only with the lælia and cattleya tribes, but also in the creation of the magnificent trigeneric sophrolæliocattleya and quadrigeneric Potinara hybrids. The open, flat shape of the sepals and petals of the *Sophronitis grandiflora* have further contributed towards the success of these multigeneric hybrids and its presence and influence are much in evidence in cattleya collections.

Sophronitis grandiflora is the most distinguished of the tribe, with larger flowers, up to 3 inches across, of a bright scarlet-red, carried singly on short stems, occasionally in twos. Growing at altitudes of 3,000 to over 4,000 feet on the Organ Mountains of Brazil, this beautiful epiphyte likes the cooler conditions of the odontoglossum house, provided a light position near the roof glass can be found for it. If grown in pots, use the potting mixture recommended for cattleyas, but use longer fibres and full-length sphagnum when grown on pieces of bark. In the latter case frequent dipping or spraying is required during the growing season, when the compost should be kept reasonably moist. This gem occupies a negligible amount of space with its 1-inch pseudo-bulbs and 2 to 3-inch leaves, and should therefore find a place in every collection.

Vanda

These monopodial epiphytes have a wide distribution ranging from North India and Burma through the tropical East Asiatic countries to beyond the Philippines, in a variety of climates which it would be impossible to reproduce in a single house. They are all lovers of light, warm and airy conditions and to flower well and regularly require plenty of atmospheric moisture when in growth, but drier, airier conditions when at rest. To say that they are easy to grow would be stretching one's imagination and should only be attempted by growers of experience who can attend to them at any time of the day, and own large, roomy, houses. Unless ideal conditions and expert treatment are provided, a vanda can grow for years without producing a single flower, and in our climate this genus has provided more disappointments than any other dealt with in this book. They seldom do well in a mixed collection, and even in the cattleya house the site for vandas has to be carefully chosen if they are expected to justify the space and attention required.

Where suitable conditions can be provided, the effort of growing these aristocrats of the orchid world is amply rewarded, as a well-furnished spike of from twelve to eighteen large and graceful flowers is something to be proud of. Whether grown in pots or baskets, they must be suspended near the roof, where they

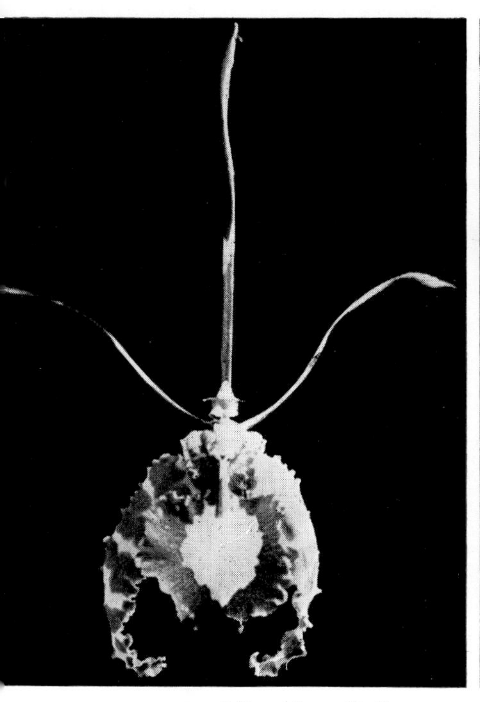

PLATE LXVIII. Oncidium "Papilio"

PLATE LXIX. Vanda "Suavis"

PLATE LXX. Bifrenaria "Harrisoniae"

PLATE LXXI

Zygopetalum "Mackayi"

PLATE LXXII (*right*)

Vuylstekeara "Jacqueline," var. Jules Verne

PLATE LXXIII

Vuylstekeara "Edna," Stamperland var.

can get all the light that can safely be admitted and where the aerial roots have a free and unobstructed run. The receptacle chosen must be of liberal proportions to hold as many roots as possible. For once, overpotting does not arise, as long as an open, well-drained compost is provided. Two parts of coarse osmunda fibre to one of sphagnum moss, with pieces of broken crocks worked in here and there, in addition to the vertically placed drainage crocks up to one-third of the pot's depth, will suit these orchids.

Water must be applied abundantly during the growing season but rather sparingly after flowering. Spraying of the whole plant with clear rainwater must be practised regularly in bright weather to supplement the atmospheric moisture, for the benefit of the aerial roots. When growing strongly (and only then), give alternate applications of manure water, preferably small pieces of dried cow manure soaked in rainwater to the colour of weak tea.

Repotting should be done once every third year. When a plant has grown too tall and straggly, or when increase of stock is desired, cut off and pot the top half of the plant. To ensure quick re-establishment of the top half, make a cut in the stem between the leaves, and wind wads of fresh, moist sphagnum moss round the cut a few months before division is intended. This will encourage the formation of new aerial roots, which should be buried in the new compost when the severed portion is potted up. The wads of sphagnum must be kept moist by spraying with clear rain-water.

The cooler-growing species listed hereafter can be grown successfully in the cattleya house.

AMESIANA. A small-growing species from Burma, with fluted terete leaves 8 to 10 inches long and 18- to 30-inch long flower scapes, sometimes branched. The flowers are fragrant, 1½ to 2 inches across; sepals and petals white with rose suffusion, the lip amethyst-purple with paler margins.

CŒRULEA. The most popular of the species, often referred to as the blue vanda, growing at high elevations in northern India and Burma, it reaches a height of 30 inches, with 6- to 9-inch leathery leaves. The flowers, up to a dozen and a half on a well-grown plant, are flat, rounded, from 3 to 4 inches across, of various shades of blue, delicately mottled with a darker shade. The sepals and petals are almost equal in size, overlapping, with narrow base; the lip small, dark blue, with white column.

KIMBALLIANA. A terete (round) leaved species from Burma, seldom growing over 12 inches high. The numerous 2-inch flowers are pure white, except for the broad lip, which has purple and yellow markings.

TERES. A tall-growing species with terete leaves, from India and Burma. Three to six colourful flowers are carried on 9- to 12-inch stems. The undulating sepals and petals are about equal in size; sepals white shaded with rose, petals deep rose or rosy magenta. The curiously but beautifully shaped and coloured fan-tailed lip is the main attraction of the flower, with purple, yellow and crimson markings.

Zygopetalum

This genus harbours several species that bear little resemblance to the true zygopetalums. The most popular species of the genus in cultivation in this country is the *Zygopetalum Mackayi* and deservedly so, with its strongly scented, attractively coloured flowers, produced up to seven in number on the upper half of the stout, erect 24- to 30-inch stem. The sepals and petals are yellowish-green with purple-brown blotches; the large, rounded lip white with violet-purple veins and spots.

A robust grower, this epiphyte from the Organ Mountains of Brazil can be grown in a mixed collection, but likes the extra light and warmth of the cattleya division. It appreciates a somewhat water-retentive compost, such as recommended for cymbidiums, which should never be allowed to dry out completely. It has two growing cycles, viz., when producing the flower spikes from the young leads and again after flowering, when developing the flowered leads into full-sized pseudobulbous growths. *Z. Mackayi* soon develops into large specimen plants, if allowed to do so, and should only be repotted to prevent overcrowding. Back-bulbs, when severed, will often produce tiny plantlets from the tops, which can be prised off when the roots are about an inch long and potted up separately. It is a good plan to pot up several of these together, well spaced out, in a shallow pan, potting on in a deeper pan or pot when it becomes necessary. In four years' time they will have reached flowering size.

Smaller-growing species with equally attractive colouring and scent are *Z. crinitum* and *Z. discolor*, whilst primary hybrids, such as *Z. Blackii* and *Z. Perrenoudii* provide deep-blue colouring as well as strong scent. All are worthy of a place in the amateur's collection.

18

RAISING SEEDLINGS FROM SEED

MANY amateurs may be tempted to enter the fascinating but extremely hazardous field of seed-raising. To make a successful cross between kindred hybrids or species may be the result of fortuitous chance, but the fact that only one in a hundred crosses made can be called successful provides plenty of food for thought.

The commercial establishments have not only generations of experience to draw on, but also possess the necessary equipment for producing seedlings the economical way—viz., the asymbiotic—pure culture—method. Various formulas for making up orchid agar are available to anyone interested, as is the specialized equipment, but supposing the amateur has successfully negotiated the many hurdles and managed to germinate, transplant and raise a few hundred seedlings, he may find after a few years of patient labours that they are only fit for the incinerator.

Space in the amateur's orchid house being what it is—a rare commodity—he will be better off by leaving three or four years of waiting in the hands of the skilled nurseryman by purchasing established seedlings of a variety of crosses. This does not necessarily mean that the keen amateur should deprive himself of the pleasure and satisfaction of trying to raise a few seedlings of his own. The symbiotic or natural way of sowing seeds will give him plenty of scope to try his skill and patience, without having to resort to chemistry. It has often been said that seedlings raised on host plants take up to twelve months less in time to mature. Although the author is not convinced of such an advantage over the pure culture method, he believes that only the most vigorous of the seed sown in a natural nutrient bed will germinate and, therefore, stand a better chance of survival.

The selection of suitable parent plants to be mated is no easy task and a second opinion, preferably by an experienced grower, should be sought. There are many factors to be considered, such as harmony of colours and patterning, size and shape of the flowers, as well as the constitution and flowering record of the plants involved. Haphazard matings are not worth the effort and loss of flowers, if not of the plants themselves, and it just is not good enough to bring two flowers together, just because they are pretty, or large. Only make crosses with a particular object in view, be it the improvement of a particular segment of the flower, be it the size of a flower, or the introduction of new colours; and always make sure that the other factors harmonize with each other. The fact that reputable hybridists spend huge sums on suitable parent plants speaks for itself. Unless the genetics of the parent plants are studied and used for guidance, the chances are that nine out of ten of the crosses made will prove sterile.

Having selected the parents, use the stronger of the two, that does not need repotting for twelve months, as the seed-bearing plant. The pollen grain should be applied to the best flower on the spike, preferably on the lower half. The seedpod will generally ripen in nine to twelve months and should be harvested when the segments of the pod start to split. Keep the pod-bearing plant in a light position and water the plant normally while the pod is forming. When the seed is harvested, you will have a weakened plant on your hands that will require careful nursing for a few months. Unless it quickly regains its former vigour, it should not be allowed to flower the following season.

It is advisable to have the seed examined under a microscope to ascertain the percentage of fertile seeds. The higher the percentage of viable seeds, the more thinly they should be sown and vice versa. Choose host plants from the same section as the parents, which must have a good surface and a compost well stocked with roots. If necessary, trim the surface level and give the plant a good soaking two hours before sowing. If you can spread the seed over half a dozen plants, so much the better—the seed may germinate on one plant and not on the other. The compost on the host plant must never be allowed to dry out and daily inspection is advised. Keeping such host plants in heated propagating frames has proved disappointing in my experience, as the confined, moisture-laden atmosphere encourages lichenous growths and algæ on the surface, which are inimical to germination and development of the seedlings.

Germination may take place in two months or two years, according to the genera involved—and a variety of circumstances. By the time your seedlings are strong enough to be transplanted into a bed of their own, your host plants will be in need of care and attention, owing to frequent waterings. Repot as soon as relieved of the seedlings and keep on the dry side and well shaded until new roots have infused fresh vigour into the plants.

The seedlings should be dibbled in finely chopped up compost of fibre and live moss in equal proportion, in small, well-crocked pots, about a dozen or so per pot. The compost must be kept moist at all times and the tiny plantlets well shaded. When the seedlings get "crowded" in their first community pot, they should be transplanted into other pots of the same size, but fewer in number, usually four or five per pot. Care must be taken to retain the old compost that adheres to the tiny roots. It will be found that some of the seedlings grow at a much faster pace than the majority of them and these can be given individual existence in separate 1½-inch pots, using the compost recommended for each genus, only finer.

At no time should the compost of seedlings be allowed to dry out and spraying of the seedlings with tepid rainwater should be practised on all bright occasions—at least until they are well rooted and established. Shading of young seedlings is as important as watering and is not likely to be overdone. Make provision for extra shading where they are grown with adult plants, otherwise stunted growth will result. How soon they will flower depends on the genus, atmospheric conditions and treatment of the seedlings and no set period can be defined, especially in view of the astounding achievements of Christopher Branch, described earlier in this book.

19

STOCKING THE WARDIAN CASE IN THE LIVING ROOM

A GREENHOUSE in the back garden is not an absolute necessity for growing orchids. A Wardian type case or glass frame installed in or near the window bay in your living or drawing room is all that is needed for growing orchids on a small scale. For such a severely restricted space it is more than ever necessary to choose the plants with great care, taking into account the temperature that can be provided all the year round. A 60-watt lamp, or an equivalent tubular element, thermostatically controlled, will provide ample heat even for a fair-sized frame. The top and front panels must be removable for easy access to the plants. The shelves should be in small, mobile sections, preferably of rust-proof open mesh, so that gaps can be left here and there for long leaves and flower spikes from the plants below.

Sufficient shading can usually be provided by adjusting the curtains. Water troughs are neither necessary nor desirable, as the evaporation from the plants in such a confined space creates ample atmospheric moisture for their needs. Ventilation must be given every day as soon as the room temperature has risen high enough to prevent chilling. The most likely cause of failure in frame culture is insufficient ventilation. Plants in flower should not be left in the frame, but taken out into the cooler, drier atmosphere of the room.

Assuming that the temperature in your frame is kept at a minimum of 65° F. at night, with a rise of 10° F. or more for part of the day, you can fill your case with the prettily mottled leaf type of cypripediums. A selection could be made from *C. Maudiæ* in variety, *barbatum*, *bellatulum*, *callosum*, *Clair de Lune*, *Curtisii*, *Lawrenceanum*, *Venustum* and others. Add to these one or two representatives of the "Jewel Orchids" and you have the most attractive indoor garden you could wish for, all the year round, whether the plants are in flower or not. If your case is high enough to accommodate 2- to 3-foot spikes, you might try the butterfly oncidiums *Papilio* and *Kramerii*, which also have attractively marked and coloured leaves. Many more oncidiums of small stature could be included, but the formation of long, often branched spikes must be allowed for.

If the night temperature of your frame hovers around 60° F., there is almost unlimited scope with green-leaved cypripediums, which should certainly include the pretty *C. Fairieanum*. *Oncidium Forbesii* and *O. ornithorhynchum*, *Masdevallias* and *Maxillarias* in variety, *Promenæa citrina*, *Sophronitis grandiflora*, *Zygopetalum crinitum*, *Z. discolor* and *Z. stapelioides* are all small, accommodating plants worth trying. A whole frame could be filled to advantage with miltonias, which, however, require plenty of ventilation in daytime.

Members of the brassia, cattleya, cymbidium, dendrobium, lycaste and odontoglossum tribes all create their particular problems and cannot be successfully mixed, apart from considerations of space, and cannot therefore be recommended for frame culture.

PLATE LXXIV
Angulocaste "Apollo,"
var. Goldcourt, F.C.C.
(*Photo: By courtesy of "Orchid Review"*)

PLATE LXXV (*right*)
Angulocaste "Tudor," F.C.C.
(*Photo: By courtesy of Wyld Court Orchids*)

PLATE LXXVI
Lycaste "Queen Elizabeth"

PLATE LXXVII

Promenaea
"Crawshayana"

PLATE LXXVIII

Oncidium
"Marshallianum"

PLATE LXXIX

Macodes "Petola" (*left*)
Anoectochilus "Sikkimensis"
(*right*)

PLATE LXXX

Mottled Leaf Cypri-
ediums (*above*) and Jewel
rchids (*below*) in Living
Room "Plantarium"

PLATE LXXXI

ame heated Glass Frame
sed for raising Seedlings
and starting Back-bulbs
into growth

PLATE LXXXII. Author's Exhibit showing Extendible Stands
(*Photo: Gardener's Chronicle*)

PLATE LXXXIII. The Author with Part of his Collection. October 1955

20

EXHIBITING ORCHIDS

WHEN the amateur has achieved a certain amount of success with his orchids, the desire for exhibiting his achievements in public follows in its wake. As most orchids flower during the cold winter months and in the early spring, exhibitions for orchids fall in that period. This often means that plants have to be taken out of their warm, sheltered quarters into the inclement atmosphere of the open road on their way to a possibly chilly exhibition hall, where they may be kept for two or three days before facing the hazards of the weather again on their return journey. That such shock-treatment does not help the future development of the plants involved, is obvious. Fortunately, there are quite a few things we can do to soften the ordeal of such plants—even to the extent of the plants remaining utterly unaffected.

Even the warmth-loving cypripediums, like the one I exhibited in January, in February and again in March, grown in a minimal temperature of 60°, will stand these occasional sorties without visible detriment, provided the normal precautions are taken. I have little regard for the excuse made by some of the amateurs for not exhibiting at orchid shows, that their plants may come to harm. After all, there would be nothing for them to see if others refused to take the risk. Naturally, a plant grown in a comparatively high temperature should not suddenly be exposed to chilly winds. My practice is to place plants to be exhibited, in the coolest section, two days before showing and then to lower the temperature of the house for the night preceding the show. If the plants can be boxed up, so much the better, but this usually involves a major operation and, more often than not, the boxes are either too large or too small. The simplest way is to stand the pots in shallow boxes with firm bottoms, arranging the plants so that they do not get in one another's way, and force newspaper between the pots to secure them firmly. The plants are then draped with a sheet of brown paper, tied to the highest stakes (special stakes may have to be provided for this purpose) and pinned to the sides of the box with drawing pins. This precaution will keep out wind and rain and has proved sufficient protection for preventing damage to the blooms and leaves during the journey. When plants are conveyed by saloon car, remember that a number of small boxes are easier to handle than one or two large boxes which have to be squeezed through the doors. If the weather is very cold, I let the engine run for 15 minutes, with the heater switched on, before transferring the plants to the car.

When plants are returned to their living quarters, the gradual re-introduction to the higher temperature is, in my opinion, even more important than the reverse process of hardening off. The generating system of the plant receives too much of a stimulus when suddenly placed in a high temperature in a quiescent condition, to return to its normal rate of development, and the subsequent "hangover" may be a long time to wear off.

It is safer to provide temporary stakes to protect the blooms in transit than to "wrap" them up. The novice has a natural disinclination to push stakes into the compost, expecting to pierce half the roots on his plants. Provided the stakes are bluntly pointed, the roots are normally pushed out of their path and it will be in the nature of an accident if a single root is damaged. As most roots congregate round the side of the pot, the stakes should be pushed in as near the centre of the pot as possible. All temporary stakes should be removed once the plant is in position on the show-bench and the permanent stakes, to which the flowers are tied, kept as short as possible.

New labels should be provided, with the genus and name of the plants clearly printed for everyone to see and read without having to pull out the label every time identification is desired. The label inside the pot-edge is not so likely to miss the roots as is a stake near the centre, especially if returned to different places.

Mossing-up, *i.e.* covering the pots and surface of the plants with moss, is a time-honoured practice and quite indispensable for the exhibitor of large groups. Unsightly props, used to bring the inflorescences to the desired level, or for tilting plants where necessary, can thus be entirely hidden under the moss. To the amateur with but a dozen plants or less to show, mossing-up is an unmitigated nuisance and hardly worth the bother. Clean pots are not unsightly and a few painted, or bright metal extendible stands, is all he needs to bring the flowers to the desired level on the show-bench. Old, cracked or chipped pots should be replaced by new ones of the same size. This should be done a few days before the show, as the plants must be soaked in water before their transfer into new pots, to avoid root-damage, and the compost should be reasonably dry before the plants are taken out of their warm quarters.

The leaves should be wiped with a wad of cotton-wool, dipped in clear rain water. If a few drops of lemon oil are added to the rain water, it will give the leaves that polished, glossy appearance, in itself very attractive.

A few foliage plants placed among the orchids will help to fill the open spaces and to avoid too much pot being shown. Except those used for background, such plants should be on the short side, certainly below the level of the flowers. Adiantums, asparagus, begonia rex and some of the cycads make excellent and contrasting "space-fillers," but many other kinds can be used to equal advantage.

APPENDIX

ORCHID RAISERS AND EXPORTERS

ARMSTRONG AND BROWN, Orchidhurst, Sandhurst Park, Tunbridge Wells, Kent.

BLACK AND FLORY LTD., Orchid Nurseries, Slough, Bucks.

A. G. BOND, Tattlebury Gardens, Goudhurst, Kent.

BURNHAM NURSERIES LTD., Kingsteignton, Newton Abbot, South Devon.

CHARLESWORTH AND CO. LTD., Haywards Heath, Sussex.

H. DIXON AND SONS, Spencer Park Nursery, Wandsworth Common, London, S.W.18.

DORSET ORCHIDS LTD., Plush, Dorset.

S. FARNES, Ashcroft, London Road, East Grinstead, Sussex.

A. J. KEELING AND SONS, Grange Nurseries, Westgate Hill, Bradford, Yorks.

STUART LOW (BENENDEN) LTD., Jarvis Brook, Crowborough, Sussex.

MCBEANS' ORCHIDS LTD., Cooksbridge, Sussex.

MANSELL AND HATCHER LTD., Cragg Wood Nurseries, Rawdon, nr. Leeds, Yorks.

R. Y. E. RATCLIFFE, Downlands Nurseries, Chilton, Didcot, Berks.

SANDERS (ST. ALBANS) LTD., The Royal Orchid Nurseries, St. Albans, Herts.

WYLD COURT ORCHIDS, Hampstead-Norris, Newbury, Berks.

INDEX